GIVE IT WELLY
Carry On Gardening

*to judy
Best wishes Caroline C*

Caroline Currie
Blue Check Books

Published by Blue Check Books, Salisbury
www.bluecheckbooks.co.uk
email: info@bluecheckbooks.co.uk

ISBN 978-0-9571124-1-4

Layout and design by Eddie Hams

Printed by Pardy (& Son) Printers Ltd., Ringwood, Hampshire

WHAT READERS SAID ABOUT
A Spade Is A Spade:
The Down To Earth Garden Book

"Quirky, confident, funny" – Keith

"Pickupable. Irresistible'" – Daphne

"From the first page you're friends with the author" – Paula

Introduction

Hello, fellow gardeners. How was your year?

Last year saw the publication of *A Spade Is A Spade: The Down To Earth Garden Book*, which revealed my struggles with the unmentionables to make the most of 2010/11 in the weed-stricken wilderness I laughingly call a garden. Some of you bought it, and now, blame yourselves, here is book No.2: *Give It Welly – Carry On Gardening*, written, like its predecessor, in ordinary language by an ordinary gardener. This time we concentrate on one topical subject per month, learn a bit about it and find tips and top favourites from local experts in wild flowers, camellias, clematis, blossom and fruit trees, roses, herbaceous borders, allotments, autumn colours, and tulips. My own ridiculous hints include the improper use of clothes pegs and litter trays, I confess How Not To Garden, let my favourite jam recipes out of captivity, and list a few more Jobs To Do, bad luck. If you get as far as December, you'll find Dig Deeper – Any Questions? You've sent me some excellent ones, which I have done my best to answer.

As I sit here under the pear tree, surveying the nasturtiums rendered leafless by the Cabbage White caterpillars, and being surveyed by Jackson, the new black and white king of the jungle, I wish you all well and hope you have a bit of gardening fun with this. Do write and tell me how you get on.

Caroline Currie
Salisbury
September 2012

Acknowledgments

Thank you Sara Carnegie-Brown, Nicky Howard-Jones, Angela Evans, Gillian Harwood, Sally Neale, Stephanie Donaldson, Joel Wilson, Sara Reeve-Tucker, Daphne Young, Sarah James, Chris Holladay, Miranda and Adam Carter, Daphne Middleton, Jenny Newman, Anne Noble, George Robbins, Andrea Caro, John Gault, Gus & Vanessa Shield, Caroline Davidson-Brewer, Michele White, Mary Luckham, Julie Horne, Sue Newman, Jackie Stoodley, Sally Vander, Keith Robinson, Anne Johns, and Jane Simpson at Waterstones, Salisbury; everyone at Waterstones is so encouraging. Heartfelt thanks to expert contributors Courtens Garden Centre, Colin Hayman, Landford Trees, Longstock Park Nursery, Charlotte Moreton (who also provided the camellia and blossom drawings for March and May), Nightingale Nursery, Pococks Roses, Harry Theobald and Trehane Nursery. The Christopher Lloyd quotations are from *Cuttings: A Year In The Garden With Christopher Lloyd,* by Christopher Lloyd, published by Chatto & Windus, and reprinted by kind permission of The Random House Group Limited. The woodcuts are from *Plant And Floral Woodcuts For Designers And Craftsmen,* by Carolus Clusius, and *1800 Woodcuts by Thomas Bewick And His School,* edited by Blanche Cirker, both published by Dover Publications Inc, New York. I would also like to thank my nephew Hugo Currie, who set up the Blue Check Books website and email, and Eddie Hams, who designed and typeset *Give It Welly,* in conjunction with Pardy (& Son) Printers Ltd.

Contents

JANUARY

Another New Year

TODAY IS THE FIRST DAY of the rest of your life. Socrates? Cicero? One of those old toga guys who crop up in crosswords. I loathe the symbolism of the New Year, it's just a day like any other. But rather than make useless resolutions to give up chocolate or sugar or booze, which last about five minutes, January 1st is a good day to look out of the window and think. A walk around the garden will get your brain into gear, and send the blood crawling, if not coursing.

It's a good month for gardening housekeeping, tedious though it is, like the indoor sort: getting the mower serviced, clearing out the shed, scrubbing, oiling and sharpening your tools. Tidy up, chuck out, sweep and wash the floor. I must confess a fascination with litter trays: I have them all over the shed, neatly containing string, gloves, weedkillery things, tins of paint, decorators' bits of stuff, electricals etc, and they are equally useful for carting plants around, and in that hellhole, the under sink cupboard. They come in jolly colours and are very cheap.

They're even useful when you clean out the pond. Hideous job, I know, but have another look at the title of this book: I never promised you a rose garden. Roll up your sleeves, and put on your Marigolds. You'd better get a move on before the frogs get that twinkle in the eye. Drag out all the fomenting foliage, leave it in a litter tray for wildlife to crawl out, empty the water if you can, scrub as much of the bottom as you can reach (be careful, I met a man on the bus who had slipped and broken his wrist), and refill with rain water. You also need to scrub the slimy stepping stones used by the frogs to climb out. How worthy (and wet) you will feel when you've done that. Treat yourself to a hot cider vinegar and honey.

Such physical labour can often give birth to good plans. How about resolving that "your garden should not go to pieces after the end of July", as Christopher Lloyd, The God of Gardening, advised. He's a good man to get you thinking. What changes and improvements can you make? This is a good question to consider from a train, looking out at other people's back gardens. Jot down a few notes. Are you bored with that shrub? Has it outgrown its space? Are the day lilies too crowded and have stopped flowering?

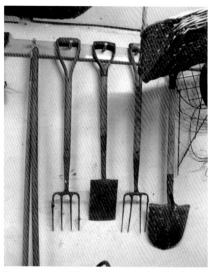

Add interest with an occasional swan?   Brace yourself to clear out the shed.

How much space would be gained, I wondered last autumn, by chopping down that overgrown half dead ceanothus and planting smelly white *Rosa rugosas* there? It warms the frozen cockles to imagine how those five new ones will look in barely four months' time, and to wonder which clematis would look good growing beside them. "The key is never to think of plants in isolation, but always in some combination. That's where the art of gardening comes in." The God was constantly trying new plantings and colour combinations at Great Dixter, and it's exciting to rethink areas of the garden every year. I find once I start, I can't stop. That first hack back, dig up, tip trip, hurl into the skip is so liberating I can hardly wait to get home and attack something else.

The God, as usual, summed it up. Advocating the thinning of old roses, he said: "Humans are expected to look after their old, however tiresome, but the same principle should not be applied to plants."

My friend Sara was in a dilemma over her 12ft length of wall against which she had planted pyracantha, three climbing roses, a *Clematis armandii,* and a *Viburnum tinus.* "What can I do?" she said, "They're all growing into each other. I know I've made a cockup. I really wanted a *Clematis armandii,* but it's such a bully." My answer was: "What makes you smile? What do you like best?" "I want a wall of roses," she said. So I suggested she should consider their needs first, and gradually eliminate other stuff. She agreed, and is now in the process of reluctant removals.

For inspiration, hop down to the library or Waterstones and see what they've got in the way of garden design books – John Brookes's are good ones. Meanwhile, here are some ideas for changes that I've found useful:

- **Add height** with a pergola, an arch or trellis on a fence.

- **Dig up the scrubby old patch of lawn** and pave or gravel.

- **Dig up some paving stones** and make small beds: too much stone can be a little bleak.

- **Re-stain fences** etc to liven up and preserve wood longer.

- **Remember rain** needs to drain away, so if paving lay on sand not cement.

- **Prune apples and crab apples** while dormant, also lilacs.

- If you're thinking big and want to **redesign your garden,** now is the best time to hold that thought and get going. Time is of the essence. If it's going to be torn apart with diggers, do it before things get growing, say March at the absolute latest.

- If making new sloping flowerbeds, **edge them high enough,** maybe with bricks on their sides, so the earth doesn't cascade off onto the path or lawn.

- **Add interest** and focal points to your garden with statuary and worked stones – reclamation yards can be an inspiration. No, I don't mean reconstituted stone virgins. <u>Please.</u> Readers of this book would not sink that low.

Need motivation? My friend Steph had an elderly Suffolk acquaintance who had a simple rule to get garden jobs done: "I decide on a daily basis to put 15 minutes aside for a specific garden job, like tidying up the canes. Extraordinary how much I can achieve."

That's an excellent principle. I call them procedures, and try to split jobs into half hours. This was Jenny the physio's suggestion when I screwed up my back digging daisies out of a customer's clay soil and had to submit myself to her tender mercies. "Never do anything for longer than half an hour," she said, "particularly digging." Try it as a NY resolution.

And for another, for tea on a bleak January day, when you come in from the garden, why not try making **Mrs Mary Luckham's first prize winning Victoria sponge** with jam filling and top sprinkled with caster sugar 8 inch (203mm) from the Salisbury Allotments summer show:

"Weigh the eggs – and weigh out equivalent amounts of flour, Stork (not butter) and sugar. Cream sugar and margarine really well till white and fluffy. (Waitrose Clarence Court brown medium eggs, with orange yolks, are the best.) Add eggs one at a time. Fold flour in with a metal spoon, gently, don't be rough.

Always line the bottom of the two tins with greaseproof – and pour an equal amount of the mixture into each. If using conventional oven, set at 180C (fan 170C) and look at it after 20 minutes, without opening the door. It might be done. 25 minutes for an 8 inch would be enough. Tip out of tin right away, bang. Use the best strawberry jam for the middle."

The improper use of clothes pegs

I use my multicoloured basketful for pegging my sheets to the line, sure, but also as colour coding snapped onto pots, for lavender cuttings (white, mauve), seeds (white for Cosmos, yellow or red wallflowers), and last year a red for the only surviving penstemon cutting. It is a useful short cut to remembering what's what and saves stuffing in a label. I also use them to attach fleece to the fence for pulling down at night to cover peach blossom, and this year to fasten it around the camellias when we went through a frosty spell.

Saving water

January is a good month to join the Smug brigade and install more water butts. It won't be long – it happens every year – before everyone is talking about drought, yawn, and hosepipe bans, while the rain pours down. Sensible Wessex Water won't hear of them, but last year put out a full-page ad in the *Journal*, suggesting how we save water. All the usual: don't keep the tap running while cleaning your teeth, use washing-up water, and a new one, save water while it's warming up. How? Two blue buckets stand in my shower, both getting nearly full until it's hot enough for me to get in and keep them company. A small amount of soap is no problem. I take them downstairs and tip them over the plants that most need water – fruiting trees, transplants, pots, stuff growing under the eaves. If the ground is already soaked I empty them into a big unconnected butt for future droughty service. I also collect rainwater in buckets at the bottom of the garden and that goes into another unconnected water butt. Six more are attached to every downpipe on the house, shed and garage. That makes eight, and I use every drop in dry times. Yes, I am Smug president, but it is sometimes exceptionally boring to have to totter round the house with a full washing-up bowl, and not simply chuck it down the drain. I never have a bath nowadays, because it means bucketing the whole thing out, though I gather you can do it sucking on a hose out of the window. Thank you, Wessex Water, I accept the golden hosepipe award.

Equally, don't waste coffee grounds. Sluice the coffee pot with water and throw over any plant – they all appreciate a caffeine buzz.

——— JOBS FOR JANUARY ———

- **Clean out the pond.**

- **Clear out the shed.**

- **Read Christopher Lloyd for inspiration.** Among many others, *Cuttings* paperback, published by Pimlico, £14.99, is excellent.

- **Dig when you can, so frost can help aerate soil.**

- **Keep an eye on broad beans, cover if frost expected.**

FEBRUARY

Wild flowers or weeds?

"THIS IS WHERE IT ALL BEGINS," I said to my friend and neighbour, Charlotte Moreton, the talented sculptor, as we were walking through the bluebells in Garston Wood near Sixpenny Handley at the end of April. Bluebells, yes, but also primroses, white wood anemones and stitchwort, violets, unfurling baby bracken, deep purple viper's bugloss and magenta common spotted orchids. We kept stopping to look, photograph and marvel at the variety. Charlotte did an ecology degree at Lancaster University: "Amazing, fabulous tutors took us out two

13

afternoons a week, we did a lot of plant spotting, hands-on ecology, identification and working out how things relate to everything else. It was exactly what I wanted to know." As for me, I had simply wandered through the fields and woods with my mother, who taught me about birds and flowers, and to my surprise their names were still there, in the dusty cupboard of memory.

We sat on a bench in a clearing and looked and listened, trying to identify the birdsong, while Charlotte's dog Raffy snuffled about in the undergrowth. So many of what grow wild are the relations of what grow tame, and my enduring affection for wild flowers means many live with me here. Starting to come out in early spring, when not much else is, they give us hope and just get on with it throughout the year, quietly increasing while more glamorous things supersede them in attracting our attention.

In February it's primroses. I can't remember how they arrived, but now they are everywhere, crazily self-seeding, particularly in the gravel paths. They don't like too much sun, and will shrivel in the heat, so shift them to dapply places, or even shady. It's easy, just water first, pull apart to split if necessary, shove them in, water, they always take to rehoming. Jackie Stoodley at Haskells, the Salisbury nursery which also has a regular stall in the market, tells me the best way to acquire primroses is to beg a plant from a friend, and wait for it to reproduce naturally, like cowslips. The proper ones – *Primula vulgaris* – don't grow well under glass, so the ones you see in garden centres are usually some form of polyanthus. Good tip, thank you, Jackie. And thank you too, Sally Vander, for saying the same applies to nerines, and lilies of the valley. "Much better to get them from someone's garden."

And bluebells, of course. They were here when I came, all over the place, Spanish, English, survivors of neglect, some struggling contorted towards the light from under rocks. Dapply places again suit them, as the woods do in April before the leaves are out. You can buy them as bulbs, *Hyacinthoides non-scripta*, but try begging for these too; some of your friends may regard them as pests and you can offer to give them a good home. Another true blue must surely be the delicious germander, 'bird's-eye', speedwell. I have a patch of it under a few lavenders, and am hoping it will spread to my lawn, which this year has been invaded by the tiny yellow-flowered slender trefoil.

I think wild flowers give a relaxed feel to a garden, and they have the great advantage on the whole of not being eaten by

Sarah's favourite wild flower – Queen Anne's Lace.

Another favourite – the yellow Welsh poppy.

somebody. There is a limit, however. When does a wild flower become a weed? My neighbour Beryl was horrified to discover her lawn being taken over by a mat of rust-coloured hawkbit, probably a cultivated escapee, that had spread so fast it threatened to obliterate the grass altogether. You have to keep an eye on weeds, and grab 'em while they're small and young. One of the very few advantages of this total pants summer is that it is so easy to pull them up. I was struck with that deep philosophy as I was crouching in the path, removing oxeye daisies. This last paragraph has been written in July, when the full horror of the rains has been with us for so long, and so many things have failed to germinate or thrive, have got blight, died, or been devoured. The plums and the gooseberries are splitting as they ripen, and the plums are rotting on the tree. What next, a plague of frogs?

Back to wild flowers: my top three:

1. **Primrose, *Primula vulgaris:*** wouldn't be without them. If you want to colonise, ask me for one of mine.

2. **Common red poppy, or Flanders poppy, *Papaver rhoeas:*** Simple, unpredictable, forever associated with the battlefields of France, and the cornfields of England. It turns up when and where it wants to, but hardly ever if you sow it on purpose. This is a 'wild' flower, with a mind of its own.

3. **Foxgloves, *Digitalis purpurea:*** handsome, upright, in purple, pale mauve or white, this one will reappear whenever you pull it up and scatter its seed. First year you'll get a rosette of leaves, in the second a flowering stem.

Charlotte Moreton's top three:

1. **Gorse, *Ulex europaeus:*** "Out now in February, the coconut smell transports me to a west coast of Scotland, Cornwall, or Wales, a rocky shore with lots of rain, lots of sea and white shell sand. That rich buttery-yellow colour looks amazing against blue skies. Even if it's not blue, the yellow makes you think it is."

2. **Dog rose, *Rosa canina:*** "The fragility, the delicacy, that perfection is so transient, makes it precious like a jewel, like a beautiful porcelain thing. And the smell: one good sniff makes you feel like your face is clean." The palest of pinks wild rose comes out in June. The *canina* comes from the Latin for dog, meaning it is a common (or valueless) flower.

3. Bog asphodel, *Narthecium ossifragum:* "A strong architectural shape, with iris-like leaves and strong lines – other plants about it are more fuzzy. Stands bolt upright with star flowers, yellow with a hint of orange, a bright joyful colour. It grows in peaty bogs, the smell of which transports me to places I'd like to be. It grows with other things that are idiosyncratic, like sundew, bog cotton, and sphagnum moss. 'Fields of asphodel'."

Pure poetry, Charlotte, thank you.

Charlotte Moreton, sculptor, artist, educator, ecologist.
www.charlottemoreton.co.uk
email: info@charlottemoreton.co.uk

I asked another friend, businesswoman, restaurateur and gardener, **Gillian Harwood,** the same question: "What are your favourites?"

"My fondest memory is of water meadows full of snake's head fritillaries by the Ouse in Yorkshire, and fields of cowslips outside Leeds. You never see those now. But I do love

1. Buttercups, *Ranunculus repens.*

2. Sorrel, *Rumex Acetosa.*

3. Ox-eye daisies, *Chrysanthemum Leucanthemum.*

All growing in a field in summer. When the wind stirs over the top of the grass, they all flow together and look lovely. If there's a cow standing in it, so much the better."

Gillianharwood@busworks.co.uk

Here are framer **Sara Reeve-Tucker** and her mother **Daphne Young's** favourites:

1. **Snowdrops,** *Galanthus nivalis:* "I love driving through banks of white, it reminds me of our old house. And **Wild daffodils** – kids used to steal them." (Daphne.)

2. **Wood anemones,** *Anemone nemorosa:* "They appear to be so incredibly fragile, but when they come up among everything in woods, they hold their own. Fragility with toughness is very attractive."

3. **Bluebells,** *Hyacinthoides non-scripta:* "That blue with the very new green is the best combination ever, though the green never lasts long."

4. **Wood violets,** *Viola Riviniana:* "Spring, grassy banks in the middle of roads, country lanes."

Sara Reeve-Tucker: Sarart@hotmail.co.uk

And my painter and printmaker cousin **Sarah James:**

1. **Queen Anne's Lace,** *Daucus carota.*

2. **Bluebells,** *Hyacinthoides non-scripta.*

3. **Lesser celandines,** *Ranunculus Ficaria:* "All make the heart lift in early spring."

"I also love **primroses, vetch, violets, red campion, stitchwort, poppies red, Welsh yellow, horned, and buttercups, and foxgloves,** on and on …"

Sarah James: sjprint@hotmail.com

And engineer **Chris Holladay:**

1. **Marsh marigolds,** *Caltha palustris.*

2. **Wild roses,** *Rosa canina.*

3. **Sea holly,** *Eryngium maritimum,*

Chris Holladay: ch.modbury@gmail.com

<u>Everybody</u> loves wild flowers.

——— JOBS FOR FEBRUARY ———

- **Start to prune clematises**, the later flowering "hard prune" (on label) ones: prune above the first pair of buds, which will be obvious now, about a foot from the ground. Pull down and bag up all the dead growth above. Don't look up when you do it because those bits can rain down into your eyes. See April for more good thoughts from Graham Farmilow, the owner of Nightingale (clematis) Nursery in Romsey.

- **Prune wisteria.** "Spur prune" side shoots back to length of a finger, and tie in main stems to where you want them to go, or cut out completely. Side shoots are where they will flower.

- **Start to prune roses,** as long as it's not frosty.

- **Split clumps of snowdrops,** after flowering. Just pull them apart and replant in groups of two or three.

- **Order seeds.**

MARCH

Carry on camellias

"CAMELLIAS ARE TOO DIFFICULT," Father Keith said, as we were staring out into his newly cleared garden, discussing what he might plant where.

They're not really. Well, a bit maybe, and aren't they so glorious that they're worth a bit of trouble? Start them off right – in acid soil, or in a pot of ericaceous compost, and get into the habit of giving them the following routine attention, which will reward you as they burst into white, pink, red, striped, single, and double flowers in March (or the lesser-known autumn ones, as I

21

discovered), set off by a background of glossy dark green leaves. I walk out the back door into Camellia Alley, where mine live in pots, and watch their buds swell and colour up through the winter. I feel early things and late things are particularly valuable, because of their rarity, and worth taking a bit of trouble about.

I am a complete sucker for camellias. I can't bear to see them suffer. *La Dame Aux Camélias*, they don't call me. If I see a sad, yellow-leafed, drooping specimen sitting in a garden centre I might offer to give it a good home, as I did for the wizened, curl-ing-leaved plant with one pink and white flower I spotted, rejected because it was "the wrong colour" for the original buyer. Two I have rescued from gardens I moved to, where they were thor-oughly depressed from chalky soil and/or lack of watering, and potted them up in ericaceous. One has grown into a huge tree of single white flowers I've had to rehome several times. Another was sold to Sam, my godson, as an indoor plant, so I swapped him for a weeping fig, and it's the last to flower, with dozens of small red single blooms. It's very satisfying to see them restored to health. The cure? The right compost, the right food and lots of water.

For you botanoraks, the RHS bible says there are over 250 species, originating in the Himalayas to China, Japan and south to Indonesia, Java and Sumatra, and Hessayon describes them as "the queen of flowering shrubs", as they come out so early, keep their leaves and need no pruning. (Yes, they do.) Try to find *Camellia williamsii* varieties, as opposed to *Camellia japonica*, because the former drop their faded flowers politely on the ground. It's nice to have a name, too. "Camellia, red" is so boring.

Nine simple rules, oh dear, for easy growing of camellias:

1. **Plant in acid soil** (to find out if yours is, check if your neighbours have camellias, rhododendrons, or azaleas, which all like acid soil.) If yours is chalky, i.e. alkaline, plant in ericaceous compost in pots. I use dark green plastic ones, don't scream, they're very inconspicuous and less heavy to move. If you put them in tubs, screw on castors.

2. **Planting position** is important. Facing west or southwest is best. Facing east their flowers and buds will be burnt by the morning sun, if it's frosty, and the north and north east icy winds do them no good at all. South is too hot for spring-flowering camellias, but would be fine for autumn/winter flowering.

3. They are pretty hardy, except in the last two freezing winters, when I lost a couple, so now I confess to **wrapping their pots in bubble wrap** for the winter and swathing them in hideous ghostly shrouds of fleece if serious frost is predicted overnight. Fix with clothes pegs and peel it back in the daytime.

4. **Cover compost with chipped slate, gravel or chipped bark** – makes them easier to water and will protect the roots. Leave at least an inch of space below the tops of the pots.

5. **Water well with rainwater** (if your tap water is chalky) right up to the top of the pot a couple of times and let it sink in. Do this right through the summer. But in a dry season, if your water butt is empty, tap water is better than none. Don't let them dry out: next year's buds could drop off,

or you could kill the plant. Camellias are expensive to replace.

6. **Feed with Miracle Gro** special food for acid-loving plants every two weeks between April and the end of July, to allow the new growth to harden off before winter. You dissolve two scoops in a two gallon (nine litre) watering can, mix it up and pour it on. This helps produce the buds for the following year, and prevents the leaves yellowing from lack of iron. Or you can use Miracle Gro slow release pellets. Give one feed in April, see how they are, and if leaves are not healthily green, feed again with half the amount before the end of the month.

7. **Prune after flowering.** It's OK, they like it. *Courage, mon brave.* Keeps them a good shape. If they're in pots, cut out the branches going into the middle, to give them a nice empty centre. If they're in the garden, you don't necessarily need to do that, if you want them to bulk up, or become a hedge.

8. Prevent scale insects by **spraying with Bio Provado Ultimate Bug Killer –** under the leaves it you can, in June or July, when the scalers lay their eggs, and into September, once a month, if there is a bad infestation. Try and do it late in the evening to avoid hurting bees. It is the excreta, yuck, dripped by the insects, on which the hideous black sooty mould grows. You can clean the leaves with a small abrasive sponge and a bit of washing-up water.

9. If you find leaves nibbled at the edges, in a half-moon shape, you may have an infestation of vine weevils. **Water in vine weevil killer.** Look out for caterpillars too.

Camellia transnokoensis – "when in full flow, it's covered in flowers."
Photo © Trehane Nursery.

There, you see, what did I say? Only nine things to remember. Easy!

My top three camellias:

1. ***Camellia williamsii* 'Jury's Yellow':** yellow and white, fluffy yellow middle, wonderful looking when all out, healthy plant. Saw an avenue of them in tubs leading to a house in London – most impressive.

2. ***Camellia japonica* 'Adolphe Audusson':** red, semi-double flowers, masses of them. I felt sorry for a tall one-stem £5 specimen in a nursery a few years ago, pruned it back, no flowers the following year, but now, wow, it's a great shape and goes mad every spring.

3. *Camellia japonica* **'Lady Vansittart'**: my former mystery rejected pink and white striped, probably my favourite, kindly identified by Trehane Nursery, the camellia specialists. So pretty, so prolific, each flower slightly different, sometimes just white.

Trehane Nursery, in Wimborne, Dorset, is the top UK camellia, blueberry and azalea specialist. I drove down to visit this family firm to ask their advice, and to persuade them to tell me their three favourite camellias.

I spoke to nursery manager, **Lorraine Keets,** and owner **David Trehane,** whose mother Jennifer Trehane, wrote the camellia bible, *Camellias – A Gardener's Encyclopedia.*

Lorraine's top three:

1. *Camellia transnokoensis:* "A fantastic upright camellia species, dense clusters of flowers, white with a pink spot in the throat, bright pink buds.

   When it's in full flow it's covered in flowers."

2. *Camellia japonica* **'Takanini':** "Upright and vigorous, dark red flowers from November until March."

3. *Camellia vernalis* **'Yuletide':** "Something for Christmas time, one of the autumn-flowering camellias. Very slow growing, very compact and masses of bright red flowers. It's scented too."

And David, who like a gentleman let Lorraine go first?

"I agree with all three, but would add

4. *Camellia japonica* **'Haru-no-utena':** for its tubular shape

Camellia japonica 'Takanini' – "dark red flowers from November until March." Photo © Trehane Nursery.

and also the different colourations in the flowers, which are pink with a red flash."

Lorraine, who has been at Trehane for 31 years, added: "If you don't have acid soil, you can grow a camellia in a pot, in ericaceous compost, but don't overpot, i.e. plant it in too big a pot. Just double the size every two to three years." She told me about autumn and winter-flowering camellias, which were news to me, of which they have twelve varieties. "They need to be put in a sunny position to flower, but we don't recommend them for too far north. Feed and prune them in the same way and at the same time as spring camellias."

I very much enjoyed my trip, had such a friendly reception, and was unable to resist buying an autumn-flowering camellia, the above 'Yuletide', now sunning itself on my deck. As I visited in

August, I was also able to pick a huge punnet of fat black and delicious blueberries, which are pickable from the third week in July for about five weeks, 10 to 4. All highly recommended, as is the sticky blueberry flapjack I bought to eat on the way home. They also do a blueberry chocolate brownie: let this be my last meal and I'll die happy.

Trehane Nursery, Stapehill Road, Wimborne, Dorset BH21 7ND. Telephone: 01202 873490 www.trehane.co.uk   email: nursery@trehane.co.uk Open: Monday to Friday 8.30am to 4.30pm, weekends 10am to 4pm, February to end April, and October to mid December.

They stock over 250 different camellias and do mail order all year round, weather permitting. The main camellia selling time is between February and April, with an annual sale from the last week in March to the end of April.

——— JOBS FOR MARCH ———

- **Chop mahonia top** off after flowering.
- **Hard prune spiraeas** in early spring, i.e. February/March.
- **Hack buddleia.**
- **Buy new clematis** before they get too tall on their canes, and while there is still a good selection.
- **Dead head camellias.**
- **Split snowdrops.**
- **Prune evergreens.**

APRIL

Understanding clematis

"MANY PEOPLE ARE AFRAID of pruning clematis," Graham Farmilow of Nightingale Nursery in Romsey said, when I went to pick up this year's collection (yellow *tangutica* and purple and white 'Venosa Violacea') on Easter Saturday. "Several of our clients" (they are also landscape gardeners) "allow *tanguticas* or *orientalis* 'Bill Mackenzie' to get into a total massive mess, when all they need do is chop them to here – 6 inches – every February and pull down the dead growth. When we plant them, we tell them, but ..."

It is true. It is second only to being afraid of pruning roses. Just walking down to catch the bus my fingers itch to get at the house on the corner's chaotic yellow clem, tangled with the equally chaotic 'Seagull' white rambler.

Keep it simple, stupid: K.I.S.S. In order to prune all clems exactly the same, as Graham said above, about 6 to 8 inches from the ground, above the first pair of buds, in February, may I suggest you **only buy clems that flower from June onwards and say "Hard prune in early spring/Pruning Group 3" on the label.** They will very often be of the (usually) trouble free *viticella* family.

All these guys flower on the new growth they make each year. And that will come from the buds you are pruning above. Graham again: "If you don't prune them, they'll grow into the neighbour's garden and flower there, and what's the use of that?" In other words they will put on new growth on top of the old growth. Shambles 'r' Us.

So be kind to your clematis. If you hanker for an earlier flowering one, and have the space, try a pink or white *montana*, and you can do what you like with it – they're tough old brutes. This is really the latest month to buy all clems, before they get too tall and tangled, and while there is the biggest range available. As you kneel in the muddy soil, with the April winds playing about your ears, planting your new fellow nice and deep, shading his root area with mulch, stones, bricks or tiles, or something growing in front, tying in his delicate stems to the cane or trellis or wire, and giving him the whole nine litres in a watering can, think of the glory he will bring to that trellis in July. Anywhere you've got somewhere for something to go up, stick in a clem. Sunny heads, cool feet. And keep watering well throughout the first year.

My three favourite hard prune clems, so far still alive and doing well:

1. *C. viticella* **and** *C. viticella* **'Elvan':** massive enthusiastic climbers, will reach 12 to 15ft, millions of tiny purple bells. Need a tree, tall wall or trellis.

2. *C. viticella* **'Romantika':** big deep purple velvety flowers, 6ft high already on 18th May. Beautiful purple curtain by early July.

3. *C. texensis* **'Princess Diana':** bright pink upright bell-shaped flowers, likes to crawl (over lavender?) rather than climb.

Keep an eye on all of them, once they start to grow, particularly this month. They will need tying in or training through at frequent intervals to stop the fragile new stems flopping and breaking in the wind. It's only too easy to break them yourself, if you try to do this job with one hand or in a hurry. Feed them with sulphate of potash or rose food after pruning in February and in the autumn mulch with FYM or compost and feed with bonemeal.

Troubleshooting. The later flowering clems are usually trouble free, and by that I mean they are less susceptible to wilt than the earlier flowering ones. I asked Graham Farmilow why. "Probably because it's generally warmer and drier from late June onwards", he said with a bitter laugh, telling me how many hitherto healthy herbaceous plants were suffering from mildew in

Clematis 'Twilight' – one of Graham's Farmilow's favourites.

this year's atrocious weather. Sometimes too there will be an unexplained death, as I seem to have lost the *Clematis texensis* 'Gravetye Beauty', whose birth (and initial death due to my stupidity) I catalogued in *A Spade Is A Spade*. The second one I put in finally came good, with red bells crawling all over one of my lavenders. I hard pruned it in February, but no sign of growth so far (even as I write this para on 18th May.) If death occurs, don't plant another in the same place. "You don't know why it's died," Graham advises.

Death by wilt. I update this chapter, writing on 8th July, to report that wilt has struck the Currie clems with a vengeance. Individual stems on 'Polish Spirit', 'Jackmanii' and my new 'Venosa Violacea' have suddenly withered and gone black, in spite of Nos. 1 and 3 being *viticellas*, about which I have been so complimentary. I talked to Roger at Nightingales about it – and he says it must be something to do with the humidity of the constant rain this summer. Wilt is a bacteria which can get into a damaged stem, and there is nothing to be done about it besides chopping it down to the ground and hoping new stems will grow. You used to be able to spray it with copper fungicide, but that's no longer available.

Here are The Three Nightingales' top three clematises:

Graham Farmilow's:

1. **'Daniel Deronda':** "The best blue, holds its colour till late, bushy, with attractive new foliage." (Flowers late spring/early summer, pruning group 2, light prune.)

2. **Rehderiana:** "Pale yellow bells. There's nothing like it, everybody wants it, I can't get it, but I'm trying to get it in from Germany. It also grows over the ground, as far as 30ft, with flowers all over the place." (Flowers mid summer – late autumn, pruning group 3, hard prune.)

3. **'Twilight':** "I don't think there's another flower like it, pink and white mottled, looks like it's cut out of a book and stuck on a plant. Stays a long time." (Flowers early summer, pruning group 2, light prune.)

Caroline Farmilow's:

1. **'Hagley Hybrid':** "I'm a pink girl. This grows up a trellis by our gate, and can have about 250 blooms. It doesn't fail. In the spring I get out a pair of secateurs and just cut it down." (Flowers late summer, pruning group 3, hard prune.)

Clematis 'Sieboldii' – one of Roger's favourites.

2. **'Burma Star':** "Dark blue with red stripe, low grower, so pretty." (Flowers early summer and again in September, pruning group 2, light prune.)

3. **'H F Young':** "I've got one, very reliable. Massive lavender dinner plate blooms." (Flowers early summer, pruning group 2, light prune.)

Roger Humby's:

1. *Macropetala* **(species):** "I like blue flowers. Double, quite spiky, very hardy, problem free." (Early flowering, pruning group 1, light prune after flowering.)

2. **'Aphrodite':** "A Japanese variety, quite large flowers, very purply blue, only four petals, difficult to get hold of."

(*Clematis integrifolia,* crawler not climber. Flowers July to September, pruning group 3, hard prune.)

3. **'Sieboldii':** "So exotic, doesn't look like a clematis, more like a passion flower, white with purple centre. Very striking, needs shelter, south or west facing, not too bushy, needs help to grow through something." (*Clematis florida* 'Sieboldii'. Flowers June to August, fluffy seed heads, pruning group 3, hard prune.)

"I didn't start off doing clematis," Graham told me, "but a good friend retired and no-one else was doing them. They're labour intensive, but I love watching the way they grow from cuttings to mature plants."

Thank you, Graham, Caroline and Roger.

Nightingale Nursery, Gardeners Lane, East Wellow, Romsey, Hants, SO51 6AD. Telephone: 023 80 814350 www.nightingale-nursery.co.uk Email: info@nightingale-nursery.co.uk Open Monday to Friday 8am to 5pm Weekends March to June Specialists in Clematis, Climbers, Shrubs and Basket Plants. Clematis are priced from £6.90.

PS Babywatch: one of my *viticellas* – 'Elvan' – has had two babies, both self-seeded or perhaps layered in a pot of box it was dangling over. One died over the winter but the other is 3 feet tall and climbing up the pergola post. Next year I must discombobulate the box and replant the clem.

——— JOBS FOR APRIL ———

- **Split hostas:** their spikes are poking up now. Tip out of pot, firmly chop into sections with a spade or bread knife, and replant in John Innes No. 3 with a handful of bonemeal, and top with grit. Water well before and after. (Thanks Mr Montybraces for this. I now have three for the price of one.)

- **Prune late season flowering plants** like caryopteris, perovskia, penstemon, ceratostigma, fuchsia and hydrangea.

- **Prune winter-flowering honeysuckle and any other winter-flowering shrub,** like daphne and forsythia. Tidy up flowered branches and cut one major stem down to the ground.

- **Finish planting out potatoes:** 6 inches deep, 12 inches apart, rows 18 inches apart. Water bottom of hole if dry.

- **Sow French beans** (upright or on their sides) in old loo rolls on window sill.

- **Prune camellias**, if they've finished flowering. Usual process: clear out interior branches and prune exterior to whatever height looks best, (and all sing together) **above an outside bud.**

- **Beware lily beetles:** red for danger. Squash 'em.

- **Buy new clematis.**

Red lily beetle – beware this month and also in August.

Peach blossom: cover with fleece on frosty nights.

Common spotted orchid and bluebell.

The coconut smell of gorse transports Charlotte to white shell sand beaches.

The dog rose, *Rosa canina*, "like a beautiful porcelain thing."

Flanders poppies, forever associated with the battlefields of France and the corn-fields of England.

Lights! Camera! Action! Close-up on 'Lady Vansittart', my favourite camellia.

Camellia japonica 'Haru-no-utena' – David Trehane's favourite. Photo © Trehane Nursery.

Camellia vernalis 'Yuletide' – "something for Christmas time." Photo © Trehane Nursery.

Trehane Nursery also specialise in blue-berries.

This unknown camellia flowers well into May.

Roger's top clematis, *Macropetala* – "hardy, problem free."

Clematis 'Daniel Deronda' – "the best blue."

'Arabella' is happy climbing through a philadelphus.

Malus transitoria – joint favourite of Ed Sanger and Christopher Pilkington of Landford Trees – "fireworks in spring." Photo © Ed Sanger.

Malus hupehensis – "heralds the arrival of a new summer." Photo © Ed Sanger

A wanton rose, 'Tuscany Superb', admired by Jackson.

'Alissar, Princess of Phoenicia' rose – "something new, a bit exciting." Photo ©
Pococks Roses.

'Chandos Beauty' – "fantastic scent, very free flowerer, a Harkness rose." Photo ©
Pococks Roses.

'The Duchess of Cornwall' – "such an easy rose to grow, masses and masses of scented flowers." Photo © Pococks Roses.

'Love and Peace' – Rebecca Pocock's No.1 choice – "a lovely cut flower." Photo © Pococks Roses.

MAY

"Blossom by blossom the spring begins"

S O WROTE SWINBURNE. Maytime. What does that conjure up? Jeanette MacDonald and Nelson Eddy. Casting clouts. Maypoles. Darling Buds. I rang Sara: "Blossom", she said. "Great fluffy pink cotton wool blossom." And I so agree. Nothing lifts the heart as much on a sunny May (or late April) morning as driving through avenues of pink sugared almond or wild white cherry blossom.

45

"Great fluffy cotton wool blossom" – *Prunus avium* 'Plena'.

May is such a gorgeous month I'd like it to last twice as long. The days are mellowing, the laburnum's yellowing, and the lilacs are about to burst forth. Sara again: "It's the acid green of hedges, young growth, hope: lovely long summer days ahead. I can't keep pace with the garden, everything has grown another foot overnight, but at last all my plant supports are hidden."

The blossom trees I know are working fruit trees. I have not been a fan of ornamental blossomers, they have a rather naff reputation, as in those prissy little pink pillars or weeping dwarves you see in people's front gardens. All are *Prunus* something or other. I am not a fan of miniatures. Size here, I think, is everything. There is a spectacular pink blossom tree in Coombe Road, Salisbury, on the way to the hospital, by Britford Lane, which almost makes me forgive it for weeping. And I photographed the handsome double white cherry on the Castle Street roundabout, which **Landford Trees**, our excellent local tree nursery, say is *Prunus avium* 'Plena' – the double version of the genus English wild cherry.

We'll come to their recommendations in a minute, but meantime, almost breaking into a Viennese polka, I have been out exploring at the garden centres, to see if I can find some flowering trees which might deschmalzify the André Rieu concert feeling of pastel pinkness. Do you know him yet? His shows are sugary but strangely compulsive, like eating a whole box of Turkish delight, and the 64 year-old Dutch violinist is rather sexy in an odd sort of way.

Catching pneumonia in the rain, I visited Country Gardens in Netherhampton Road, Salisbury, and Wilton Garden Centre. There was not a lot of choice: at Wilton, *Prunus* 'Amanogawa' was pale petticoat pink, and there were a number of (miniature) "flagpole" cherries. Country Gardens' brightest pinks were a small *Malus* flagpole crab apple, 'Ballerina', a proper height *Malus* x *moerlandsii* 'Profusion', and 'Golden Hornet' crab had pretty white flowers. (Tip from Nicky at Country Gardens: trees in flower sell out fast, for obvious reasons, so if you're thinking of getting one, hurry along mid April to mid May to get the best choice.)

'Bramley' apple blossom – a working fruit tree.

Coming back I stopped in the rain to photograph the impressive row of pink blossom trees along Netherhampton Road. This was the nearest I got to Japan this year, where blossom time – *hanami* – is a huge tradition. It takes place throughout the country, from the end of March to the middle of April, depending on location and weather. This is mostly cherry blossom (though they give no IDs) – *sakura* – or plum blossom – *ume*. To the Japanese they are a metaphor for life – beautiful but ephemeral – as the flowers only last two weeks.

Yeah, indeed. And the rest of the year? Do we despise something beautiful but ephemeral? Paeonies, for example, irises, day lilies, oriental poppies – all come and go in an instant. As for blossom trees, it's still a bit too André Rieu for me, but if you have a passion for pink knickers, or room for a decent height ornamental flowerer, fine. Otherwise, perhaps best to admire other people's, fly to Tokyo, and get yourself a fruit tree that will earn its keep with flowers that bloom in the spring tra la, and pears, peaches, plums, apples, greengages, crab apples and damsons that you can pick and eat or stew or pie or crumble or turn into jellies and chutneys (see October.)

But don't listen to me. Let's see what the experts say. I went to see **Ed Stanger and Christopher Pilkington at Landford Trees**, and asked them for their favourite three blossom trees:

Ed Stanger's Top Three:

1. *Malus hupehensis:* "Scented crab apple with large, pure white flowers, heralds the arrival of a new summer."

2. *Malus transitoria:* "Soft pink in bud, then a mass of star-shaped flowers."

3. *Prunus* **'Shirotae':** "Nice pure white flowering cherry. When you see its white blossom against the blue sky, you know spring is truly here."

Christopher Pilkington's Top Three:

1. *Malus transitoria:* "The same as Ed. We specialise in *Malus* here - we have 110 varieties. Fireworks in spring,

smallish white blossom, little bit of pale green leaf, autumn colour orangey, little yellow fruits."

2. **'May'** – *Crataegus* **'Rosea Flore Pleno'** – "The common pink-flowered hawthorn, comes into flower after the *Prunus* and *Malus* seasons, red fruits in autumn, a tough customer that doesn't let you down."

3. *Pyrus salicifolia* **'Pendula':**   "The weeping silver-leaved pear. It's always been top of the pops on a lot of people's lists, the grey foliage looks wonderful against a yew hedge, white flowers, mid blossom season, can be clipped."

Thank you Ed and Christopher. So two of Ed's favourites, and one of Christopher's, are crab apples, or as they describe them, flowering crabs. Ed told me of many hitherto unknown to me, which also produce fruit for jelly making: "'Jelly King', 'Pink Glow', *kansuensis* (scented, reasonable sized fruit), 'Laura' and 'Harry Baker'. The most well-known in the past has been 'John Downie', but it is disease prone." Most of these, and numerous others, are available from Landford Trees. Currently a light standard, 9ft to 10ft tall, would cost in the region of £30 + VAT.

Landford Trees, Landford Lodge, Landford, Salisbury SP5 2EH. Tel: 01794 390808. www.landfordtrees.co.uk Email: trees@landfordtrees.co.uk Open: Monday to Thursday 8am to 5pm, Friday 8am to 4pm.

On the A36 near Salisbury, Landford Trees have a huge selection of trees of all sorts, and they really know what they're talking about. I bought my 'step-over' espaliered apples from them.

How not to garden: An author's tale

I sinned on Sunday. I went up to Country Gardens (née Flower-land) to buy some marigold seeds, and found a sad, unsupported apple tree, in the half price row. It was a 'James Grieve', one of my favourite eaters, £10, six feet tall, with tiny apples, and was loose in its pot, waving in the wind, unwatered, unloved. Oh dear, and there were three pears as well. I felt so sorry for it, I bought it, on impulse, something I say we gardeners should never do. What, never? Hardly ever.

With difficulty I loaded it into the passenger seat, head first, seat belt on, and when home I shoved it in a bucket of water and tied it to the soil pipe, while I considered the big question: location, location, location.

Three hours later 'James G' was installed in my lawn, lashed between a stake and an old fork, lavishly watered, and I was slumped in a chair, exhausted. I go out every day to inspect him, and currently he is the daily recipient of a bucket of shower water, as is Father Keith's greengage, given me by the rector, both fruiting trees a priority, along with the apples, the peach and the two pears. I now have a bit of an orchard. I hope he will survive, as when I turned him out of his pot most of the compost fell off, and he was left with very little around his roots. Please, garden centres, take care of your plants. CG had a number of miniature peach trees, all completely contorted by peach leaf curl. Who's going to buy them like that? Cruelty to plants, my cousin Sue calls it. RSPCP. Sometimes they seem to be crying out for help.

Sometimes we need to sin.

——— JOBS FOR MAY ———

- **Prune camellias,** if they've finished flowering. See April.

- **Plant seeds outdoors** and hope for the best. Poppies, cornflowers, marigolds, morning glories.

- **Put out bedding plants,** if you must, after 21st May.

- **Cut evergreen grasses back or split.** This year I just trimmed the dead ends, like a hairdresser, about four to six inches. Looks better and encourages new growth.

- **Keep an eye on gooseberries,** now with tiny ones showing, the tips can suddenly curl with green or black fly. Spray if necessary with Bio Provado Ultimate Bug Killer, late in the evening.

- **Keep an eye on boxes.** Mine have white fly again. Spray as above.

- **Do you have a slimy deck or paving stones?** Dangerous. You can no longer avoid this Herculean task. Brace yourselves for a pressure hose or scrubbing brush.

STOP PRESS: compost and legionnaires disease. Just heard on the news about this possible link, especially in Scotland. God knows how it works. Use gloves, or wash hands, don't hang your face over the bag when pulling compost out, they even suggest wearing a mask, imagine.

JUNE

"The wanton roses"

THAT'S HOW WS GILBERT DESCRIBED THEM in one
of the most beautiful songs he and Arthur Sullivan wrote,
and which I seem to have been singing since I saw the Opera
North production of *Ruddigore* last winter. It tells of someone
who comes to a garden to "gather flowers, and he wanders
through its bowers, toying with the wanton roses, who, uprising
from their beds hold on high their shameless heads ... never
doubting that for Cytherean posies he would gather aught but
roses." It's sung by Mad Margaret (yes, all right, thank you).

Roses rule supreme in June. 'Wanton' is a wonderful word for them. The big ones, double ones, floppy ones, blowsy ones, fancy ones, wide open and scented to heaven, like 'Madame Isaac Pereire', 'Gloire de France', or any of the David Austin 'English Roses.' I also have a tender corner of my heart for the smaller, more modest, single maidens, like 'Yvonne Rabier', producing non-stop sprays of tiny white flowers, the April flowering 'Canary Bird' with small single, you got it, yellow flowers, and it'll do it facing north as well, as will the climber 'Madame Alfred Carrière', whose first delicate white flower appeared on my pergola a week ago, on 18th May. Hey, and don't let's forget Charlotte's favourites, the wild dog roses – *rosa canina* – scattered over the hedgerows, perhaps best loved of all.

Like coffee, roses might be an acquired taste. Maybe you grow into them. Maybe those stiff lollipop standards of my youth, marching down either side of a path, soured me, and so often rose beds are still forgettable, pale yellow and pink, nondescript, listless, in need of dead heading, covered in rust and black spot. Even yesterday, walking round admirable Abbey House Garden in Malmesbury, home of Mr and Mrs Pollard, "The Naked Gardeners", my cousin Victoria and I, with slight embarrassment, both thought the 2000 different roses, scattered like Smarties in multi-coloured rose beds, were initially impressive, but lost impact all jammed in together. One of this, one of that – it was a bit 'so what'? Sorry, Mr Pollard, who was out there in blue lycra shorts (thankfully) and a bikers' T-shirt, deadheading an obelisk of 'Compassion.'

Give me the wanton type, lots of them, cascading, exploding, crawling, hurling themselves at you, "holding on high their shameless heads", begging you to bury your face in them.

As I deal with pruning roses in November, let's talk here about how to grow roses successfully. What do we need? Here are my thoughts, followed by those of excellent **Pococks Roses** in Romsey, where I buy all mine.

- **Choose a good position**, any soil, with at least four hours of sunshine a day (if there is any) in the peak growing season.

- Do not resist an urge for a rose **that makes you smile.**

- **Make sure you have enough space for it** – don't buy a 'Mermaid' unless you are prepared for it to cover the house, let alone a rambler, like 'Kiftsgate'. Study the small print. Ask advice.

- **Choose a gorgeous name.** I dare you to buy a 'Gardeners Glory', 'Cutie' or 'Honeybun', and not to blush when people ask you what it's called. I must go and lie down. (Sorry, Pococks.)

- Be happily prepared to **water, feed, prune** and occasionally spray.

- Oh, and **deadhead.** Cut to next outward-facing set of leaves.

- **Plant with care**, potted or bare-rooted. Bonemeal at bottom of hole, Rootgrow sprinkled on the roots, several handfuls of FYM or compost mixed with the soil, same level as in the pot or just below the grafting lump, water, water, a whole can full.

- **Make sure it's healthy.** Martyr to black spot is a pain, just not worth it.

My new acquaintance: As I mentioned in January, I have cleared a space in the front garden for five bare-rooted *Rosa rugosas* 'Blanc double de Coubert', and at the foot of 'Gertie' for 'Reine des Violettes' – such a lovely name – a French rose dating from 1860. The *rugosas* replace a ceanothus, grown into a tree, and the queen a large chunk of pink hardy geranium, smothering some 'Starfire' phloxes, which I split and moved. It was time for some new excitement.

My top three roses:

1. **'Gertrude Jekyll':** one of David Austin's 'English Roses', an enthusiastic, spicy sweet-scented semi-climber. One major go and then it does a bit more later on in the summer.

2. **'Constance Spry':** huge fragrant double pink climber, the epitome of 'wanton'. It flowers once and if you miss it, it's your loss, fella.

3. Console yourself with **'Bonica'**, a reliable pink modern shrub that Pococks say looks good in drifts, I believe them. I have a drift of two.

Pococks – Rebecca and Stewart – add this good advice:

● **"Don't plant roses in soil previously occupied by roses,** unless you change the soil or use a mycorrhizal fungi (Root-grow.)

● On sandy or chalky soils, you need to **feed every month**, from early March to early August." Blimey.

● **"And wash it down with 4 to 5 gallons of water"** – that's two watering cans full. I shall be a martyr to backache.

'Constance Spry' – one of my favourites. Flowers only once - sniff it while you can.

- **"Roses are OK in pots,** as long as the pots are big enough. Small roses 30cm x 30cm, medium 40 cm x 45 cm, larger roses 45cm x 60cm. J.I. No.3, Osmocote and liquid tomato feed mid July – Sept.

- **Uncle Tom's Rose Tonic** really makes a difference to the growth of roses. Water it in, or spray it on, in addition to feeding. Anecdotal evidence suggests it helps against fungal disease too. We stock it, and can't recommend it enough."

Rebecca Pocock's top three favourite roses:

1. **'Love and Peace':** "A lovely cut flower, long strong stems,

big blooms, classic hybrid tea, nice cheerful strong yellow, with a little bit of red edging on the outer petals. Not heavily thorned."

2. **'Glorious':** "Yellow, a bit thorny, a good tough bedding rose, has done very well in this awful weather."

3. **'Cinderella':** "A climber, very feminine, a pretty pink, glossy foliage, doesn't become obstreperous."

Stewart Pocock's top three:

1. **'The Duchess of Cornwall':** "Such an easy rose to grow, pinky-orange, compact, masses and masses of scented flowers, lovely shape, great for cutting, healthy, almost the perfect rose."

2. **'Chandos Beauty':** "A brilliant seller with a fantastic scent, very free flowerer, lovely colour – palest peachy blush – we've grown it for the last ten years, a Harkness rose, one of the most popular of hybrid teas."

2. **'Alissar, Princess of Phoenicia':** "One of the new series of *Rosa persica* hybrids, lovely things, this one cream, all with a dark eye blotch. Something new, a bit exciting, there's a whole new series of hybrids coming out."

All these roses are available from Pococks Roses. Stewart added, "If I go to a flower show and we sell rose after rose, that's my favourite! A lot of people get stressed about growing roses – but as long as you remember to do things in the right way, it's pure common sense and enjoyment. Feed them, and if you don't know

'Cinderella' – one of Rebecca's top three. "A very feminine climber, a pretty pink."
Photo © Pococks Roses.

about pruning, just hack them down by a third." (See November
for more about pruning.)

"As roses grow older, they become less vigorous, like humans. The colour of the flower can vary. Weather affects it, as does the condition of the soil. Flower form varies, too, according to how you grow them. If you don't prune hard enough, you won't get the shape of the flower. And if you don't feed, you won't get the quantity of flowers, and the quality and health of the plant will decline."

"It's important to get over to people how easy roses are, how good they are", Rebecca said. "They provide a lot of value in the garden. Don't be scared, you're not going to hurt them."

Pococks' top tip for keeping roses fresh in a vase: "the tiniest drop of bleach."

Pococks Roses, Jermyns Lane, Romsey, Hampshire SO51 OQA. Tel. 01794 367500. www.garden-roses.co.uk email sales@pococksroses.co.uk Open Monday to Saturday 9am to 5pm.
Bare root roses from £7.25, potted from £9.25.

———— JOBS FOR JUNE ————

- **Cut back euphorbias** before they seed.

- **Trim wisteria** as its new long whippy growths threaten to take over your house. Prune side shoots back to six inches, and leaders by a third, tying them in where appropriate.

- **Prune ceanothus,** avoiding cutting into the old wood.

- **Remove one branch at base** from late spring flowering shrubs.

JULY

Midsummer borders

"WHAT DOES JULY MEAN TO YOU?" I asked my colourful friend and former painter, Angela, in shades of brick and satsuma. "The traditional English herbaceous border," she said. "It forms the basic structure of an English garden. The pleasure of perennials: delphiniums, lupins, marguerites, echinacea, sunflowers, and hollyhocks. Colour is so important, too. Some people say anything goes, but it doesn't, in the same way it doesn't in paintings, fashion, or ceramics. There is a marvellous herbaceous border in Regent's Park, all different shades of delphiniums, from ice blue to amethyst."

61

The word herbaceous means perennial plants that die down and become dormant in the winter, reappearing in the spring. Nowadays these are often mixed with roses, evergreens, shrubs, bulbs and grasses, to form a mixed border, as in Christopher Lloyd's famous long border at Great Dixter. I agree with Angela about colours, but let's not be too tasteful, either. As The God says: "Surely a little vulgarity is in order, from time to time. There comes a stage when good taste begins to nauseate." Oh, how we miss you, Christo. Pour me a drink.

A gardener's greatest ambition might be to achieve a successful July and August border – it certainly is mine. Design and planning are key, splitting and supporting are essential, taking cuttings, battling slugs, filling gaps. Think big and dramatic, think contrasts of shapes, what goes with what, what's out when, what succeeds what. Let's start as always with one plant that makes us smile.

Hooray for the sudden thought of **Longstock Park Nursery, Stockbridge, Hants,** where I remembered an impressive herbaceous border adjoining one of the walls of the nursery next door. This is all part of the Leckford Estate, bought by Oxford Street retailer John Lewis in 1928, and now owned and managed by Waitrose. The estate also comprises the Longstock Park Water Garden, Leckford, The Waitrose Farm, and the John Spedan Lewis Trust for the advancement of the natural sciences.

"You need to talk to Alan," I was told when I rang. "He comes in on Sundays and does the border." So I made a date with him, and drove over with my camera.

As I pushed open the swirly iron gate, I saw my memory had not been wrong: it was wonderful. Colourful and dramatic, with

Brilliantly blue agapanthus in Longstock's Park Nursery's herbaceous border.

distinct different and generous groups of plants, it seemed to go on forever – apparently a total of 100 yards – divided in two by a path through to the nursery. The top bed – about 107ft as I paced it out – and 18ft deep – was mostly yellow, blue, purple and white, and the bottom bed, an unbelievable 193ft, added in hot colours, red, pink, bronze, and orange. The plants stood proud, held up by effective and discreet iron supports, obviously put in early so they barely show by July.

Gardener Alan Drewitt, whom I discovered invisible, behind a clump of *Cephalaria gigantea,* tugging out bindweed, is obviously not afraid of height. Or of numbers: "I put in five, seven, nine and sometimes eleven", he said. "You've got to put in enough plants to make a show."

The herbaceous border has been there for at least 20 years, and is intended as a display, or shop window, for the plants on sale in the nursery. Alan does indeed keep it in order on one day a week, and prides himself on it being a true herbaceous. "I love it like that. No shrubs, and the only roses are climbing up the wall at the back." He is self-employed, and has been looking after four or five other gardens, including a Gertrude Jekyll one, for at least 18 years, some for 22. He started working on the Longstock herbaceous five years ago, and also planted the lavender *angustifolia* hedges that frame the *Clematis viticella* and apple, quince and pear tunnel opposite, commenting: "Lavenders have only a six to seven year lifespan, so there's only a certain amount you can do, pruning twice a year, to prevent them getting too woody. When they do, heave them out and start again."

Walking down the border with him, we identified the main stars of the show, which I list as inspiration to us all: "Oxford blue" *Salvia patens* ("difficult to get hold of this year, tender, you need to take cuttings"); chin high *Knautia macedonica*; yellow achillea 'Moonshine'; hardy *Geranium psilostemon;* pale yellow hemerocallis; yellow heleniums; *Nepeta* 'Six Hills Giant'; white Japanese anemones 'Honorine Jobert'; maroon heuchera in front of the bed; *Cephalaria gigantea; Verbena bonariensis;* blue delphiniums ("cut down to the ground after flowering and they can come back three times"); small yellow *Kniphofia* 'Little Princess'; 'Honka' yellow dahlias with star-shaped flowers; eupatorium (late white flowers in November); bright yellow *Helianthus* 'Loddon Gold' ("can get to 6ft in a good year"); hardy geraniums in shades of mauve, 'Brookside', 'Orion' and 'Rozanne' ("don't hesitate to cut them down after flowering, and they'll come back"); white *Gaura lindheimeri;* and huge enclosures of something tall and beautiful in blue, *Salvia uliginosa*.

The bottom bed kicks off with one of my favourites, the ravishingly bronze *Heleniums* 'Moerheim Beauty'; *Anthemis tinctoria* 'E C Buxton'; 'Garnet' penstemons ("one of the hardiest, along with 'Osprey', very rare to die"); startling scarlet dahlias and also the purple-leafed 'Bishop of Llandaff'; dahlia 'Twynings After Eight'; gypsophila; apricot and pink hemerocallis; pink and mauve phloxes; bronze fennel; pink hollyhocks; pale pink *Monardas* 'Beauty of Cobham'; deep violet aconites; red hot

Cephalaria gigantea – reaching for the sky.

pokers; *Coreopsis* 'Zagreb'; astrantias; *Sedum* 'Ruby Glow'; purple tradescantia; grasses including *Stipa gigantea, Stipa tenuissima* 'Pony Tails', and two *Miscanthus,* 'Morning Light', and 'Silberfeder'; more *Cephalaria gigantea*, reaching for the sky, as were the cardoons, *Cynara cardunculus*; brilliantly blue agapanthus; *Stachys lantana*, loved by bees, as was the persicaria, or polygonum; *Potentilla* 'Gibson's Scarlet'; *Anthemis* 'Sauce Hollandaise'; *Aster* 'Lye End Beauty', "deep pink and mildew resistant"; burnet *(sanguisorba)*; and calamintha, or calamint, a big attraction to shiny green leaf beetles, bees and hoverflies.

Indeed, the whole garden seemed to be buzzing with bees and alive with birdsong – it must be bird heaven. And a wildlife paradise, although Alan might not agree while chasing out rabbits. He is a delightful, friendly chap, happy to chat to visitors walking by with cameras, while continuing to hoe, deadhead, and tuck back straying stems into their pens. He told me that he keeps the small gaps around the groups of plants for practical reasons. This is why everything stands out so well. I'm ashamed to say my Gaudy bed tends to be a mess of things growing out of a mess of grass, sort of an overgrown meadow. Oh dear, must try harder.

Alan's top three tips for a successful herbaceous border:

1. **"Regular deadheading.**

2. **"Regular hoeing.**

3. **"Watering if really dry** – but later in the season, not early. If you start and then stop, they'll die. They need to get their roots down."

And his three favourite plants?

1. *Salvia uliginosa:* "Pale blue, can be 5½ to 6ft tall. Flowers through till the end of November, can stand a light frost, I won't cut it down much, I heap a bit of compost to protect its roots, leave it in the ground and hope."

2. *Geranium* '**Rozanne**': "Normally more compact than this year, with all the rain. Flowers change colour, they start powder blue and fade to light mauve."

3. *Gaura lindheimeri* '**Whirling Butterflies**': "Lovely, flows, airy, light, ivory with a tint of pink."

"Do you feed the border, Alan?" I asked him. "Vitax Q4, in late spring, and six two-ton trailer loads of leaf mould from the woods are delivered, which I spread 2 to 4 inches thick."

The central arched avenue of fruit trees and The National Collection of *Clematis viticellas* is at its best in July, and the bed on the other side contains The National Collection of Buddleias. All these plants are on sale in the nursery, where you can also admire the Gilchrist Collection of Penstemons, formed by Kate Gilchrist and her husband, Warren, a retired director of John Lewis.

Longstock Park Nursery, Longstock Park, Stockbridge, Hants SO20 6EH. Telephone: 01264 810894.
www.longstocknursery.co.uk
email: longstocknursery@leckfordestate.co.uk
Open: Monday to Saturday 8.30am to 4.30pm all year.
Sunday 11am to 5pm March to October,
**   11am to 4pm November to February.**
Longstock Park Water Garden, in a seven-acre plot around

lakes and streams fed by the River Test, was made by John Lewis in 1943, in order to have somewhere peaceful to relax. Linked to the nursery by a 70-acre arboretum, it is open on the first and third Sundays between April and September, in aid of a different charity each time. Entrance £5. Well worth a visit.

(Longstock Park Nursery manager Harko told me they swept the board at the 2012 New Forest Show, winning the Best Show Garden Centaur Trophy, the Henry Compton Cup for Best Commercial Exhibit in Show, the Large Gold Medal and the RHS Banksian Medal. Congratulations.)

———— JOBS FOR JULY ————

- **Deadhead and feed roses** after their first flush of flowers is over.

- **Prune ramblers** after flowering. Trim back any branches you can reach, particularly those growing towards the middle. Feed. Then let this year's new branches grow, because on them will be next year's flowers.

- **Trim boxes,** if you didn't do it on Derby Day. And any other evergreens. This is the last month to do it, to allow new growth to harden off before winter.

- **Spray camellias** with Bio Provado Ultimate Bug Killer, under the leaves if you can. Do it late in the evening, to prevent hurting bees.

- **Spur prune gooseberry side shoots** to four or five leaves from base.

AUGUST

Vaudeville and the art of the Allosaurus
(Vegetables and Allotments)

AUGUST IS NORMALLY the month of 'bultitudinous' veg harvests, to use Arthur Marshall's word. Everything is growing so fast you can't eat it all, and bowls of Help Yourselves pop up on drives and doorsteps. But this year nothing is normal. Down at the allotment they are cursing the slugs, digging up their

Harry's Allosaurus plot, 13 rods, and buzzards circling overhead.

blighted potatoes, and mourning their mildewed onions. We all find comfort in our shared disasters.

ALLOTment – what an uninspiring word, and viewed from a train, they can look rather tatty, scattered with ramshackle huts like outside privies. But the other day I spotted fruit cages, green-houses, poly tunnels and cloches. "They're largely for protection," Salisbury Allotment Association's Vice Chairman, Harry Theobald, told me, when we met in the rain at his plot in London Road, Salisbury. "From pigeons and people."

Vegetables is a terrible word, too: VEGetables. It's very Eeyore-like, as are all its permutations. Let's start a policy of rechristening depressing words. Rebranding. How about VAUDEVILLE? Sparkly, entertaining, slightly lewd. And for allotment? ALLO-SAURUS: a large bipedal carnivorous dinosaur of the late Jurassic period. What do you think? I'm off to grow vaudevilles in my allosaurus, provided I like to eat them, can't buy them, they taste good, and are <u>easy.</u>

Allosauruses are marvellous assets for people who have small gardens. "My allotment saved my life," I quoted my friend Sara in *A Spade Is A Spade,* who was a vaudeville virgin before she found her patch down the road in Sussex. Helped by her grandson Hugo, she also swears by the freely given advice from her new friends Ron and ex jockey, Ken, who have dug for victory since the dawn of time.

The evening before I was due to meet Harry, my friendly allosaurus expert, I had a glass of wine with my neighbours, Gus and Vanessa. It turned out they used to have a bipedal carnivorous dinosaur, before the upkeep became too much, with Vanessa expecting her second child. Their advice for a successful one?

- **"Time.**

- **"Choose a plot near the water pump.**

- **"Loads of horse manure."**

"There are over 728 plots, in ten sites, in Salisbury", Harry told me. "There is always a waiting list, and although allotments have always had the image of old codgers saying 'in my day', nowadays all sorts of people, young, old, young families, are allotment holders. We rent them from the Council, the smallest ones are 5 rods long, though sizes are all different, at the cost of £5.75 per rod per year." 5 rods! How brilliant that a measurement so mediaeval can still exist in this decimal age. I looked it up: a rod is the same as a perch or a pole, and the equivalent is 5.0292 metres or 16.5ft. So 5 rods, the minimum length, is 82.5ft. Phew.

Harry, a seven-year veteran, has a double plot: 13 rods long by about 12ft wide. On it he grows runners, potatoes, brassicas, salads, rhubarb, onions, shallots, spinach, parsnips, carrots, and, in his impressive fruit cage, red and blackcurrants, gooseberries, blackberries, and autumn and summer raspberries. At the end of the garden is his orchard, a wildlife area with pond, and his hut, of course. Think that's all? No, he also has a greenhouse full of tomatoes, peppers and chillies. And flowers. "I have a courtyard garden so I grow those too." A dazzling display of dahlias, at their best in August, blazed out at me in the rain. "I keep them in the ground all winter, just cover them with a thick layer of straw."

"How often do you come down here, Harry?" I asked. "At least once a week, depending on the weather. If it's really hot you need to come and water every night - the water butts are linked to the water supply. It's lovely on a summer evening, lots of buzzards circling overhead."

"What about new people?" I asked him. "How do they get on?"

"They need to be prepared to dig," he said, "there is no short cut. We are plagued with creeping thistle, bindweed, and couch grass, and the only way to get rid of those is first to cut everything down to see what's there, then attack them in bite-sized pieces, covering up what you've done as you go with black polythene. The worst thing you can do is ask the Council to rotavate: this leaves bits of roots in the soil, and up the bindweed will spring again. The trouble is the TV: people are seduced by these programmes into thinking they can have instant results. There's no substitute for hard work."

Harry's advice for a successful allosaurus?

- **"Get as much advice as you can,** through books, word of mouth; don't be frightened to ask other allotment holders for advice, there is great camaraderie.

- **"Plan.** For new people it's preferable to take on a plot in the autumn, so they have the winter to plan.

- **"Build your soil up.** The more manure, compost, leaf mould you can dig into the soil, the better. Use Blood, Fish and Bone, or chicken manure pellets, to feed plants.

- **"Best to visit one hour a day over four days,** rather than one day for four hours.

- **"Have a list of essential jobs** and stick to these first.

- **"Stamp your own character on the space,** and it will add to the diversity that each person brings to the site."

The diversity in the London Road site includes sunflowers, sweet peas, gladioli, even pink echinacea. "We have a Chinese gentleman who grows Chinese veg, a lady from Zimbabwe whose family sends over seeds of African vegetables, and there's also an Indian family. It's all good."

Harry's top three favourite vaudevilles:

1. **Runners:** "Large crops up to the first frost. Easy to freeze. There is no better taste than home grown, especially when you are longing for spring to arrive."

2. **Onions:** "An essential kitchen vegetable. Can grow two crops a year from autumn sowing, followed by another in spring. They store well if dried thoroughly."

3. **Carrots:** "Can be grown all year, including winter in a heated greenhouse. A very versatile veg to use in soups and stews, or to give you a feel-good factor seeing that bright colour on your plate."

harry.theobald@btinternet.com

To apply for an Allosaurus, contact the Parks Department of your local City Council.

"A sentimental passion of a vegetable fashion"
(WS Gilbert)

My visit to St Michael's Hall, Bemerton Heath, on 11th August, for the annual show of the Salisbury Allotments Association, brought out a mixture of fascination, education, jealousy, gluttony and hysteria. On the way in, I bemoaned our mutual legumery failures with Gillian, the friendly produce stallholder, and entered the hallowed exhibition space, to be told by a slightly frosty lady that I could not buy the quiches, lemon drizzle cakes or yellow dahlias laid out so temptingly before me. (It was a show, Caroline, for God's sake.)

The heaviest cabbage must have weighed the same as my cat, Jackson, and the longest runner bean was an extraordinary 22 inches. I loved the Odd Shaped Vegetable category: "An alien's brain" potato, and a sort of introverted carrot with half a dozen legs all tangled together. Men Only Carrot Cakes looked good, as did the Cornish Pasties, Dorset Apple Cakes (Harry's won First Prize), and the Courgette and Leek Flans. How cruel that we couldn't put in a bid. They could have raised a bit

6ᵗʰ HORTICULTURAL
SHOW 2012

1st PRIZE

Prizewinning vaudevilles and fruit at the Salisbury Allotments Association show.

of cash from me that way, as they could have from Mrs Mary Luckham's prizewinning Victoria sponge – see January for the recipe.

"The young are very interested in growing vegetables, particularly organically", Mrs Luckham said. "Once they do it once they'll do it more. There is so much violence in the world, we need to encourage it. Through gardening I think you fall in love with Mother Nature." My very thoughts, Mrs L.

She also recommended her 'gorgeous' prizewinning First Earlies, 'Pink Fir Apples', which I went over to view, along with the other potato categories, Coloured and plain old White, all displayed on the requisite paper plates. Feeling as if I might bump into Lord Emsworth at any moment, I progressed to the rather sad Pair of Lettuce with roots left on, Three of any root veg, including parsnips surely 4ft long, Three tomatoes, medium, 2½ inches diameter, Three cherry tomatoes not greater than 1⅜ inches, and Pair of Marrows 13¾ inches maximum length – I'm sure 'Plum' would have had something to say about these measurements.

When I got home, my neighbour Michele White came round and told me about her pumpkins. " 'Crown Prince' are the best," she said, "duck egg blue, fantastic taste. Slice the top off, scoop the centre out, fill a third to a half with strong cheese, like mature cheddar, and chopped garlic, fill up with cream till two thirds full, bake 2 to 3 hours, 160C heat, depending on size. Serve with chunks of bread, and wine, preferably red, but we're not fussy on colour."

——— JOBS FOR AUGUST ———

- **Deadhead**, to prolong flowering; with geraniums, nip off at bottom of stalk.

- **Order/buy bulbs.** You'll get the best, fattest, firmest. Quick, before everybody else has the same idea.

- **Cut back buddleia,** chopping off about a third of each flowering branch. Be brutal, you'll need to do it again in March.

- **Chop down old loganberry canes** and tie in new ones.

Gateway to a wonderful herbaceous border at Longstock Park Nursery.

Alan's favourites: Gaura and *Geranium* 'Rozanne'.

Gardener Alan Drewitt keeps the border in order.

Allosaurus Harry at his Salisbury plot.

Harry's star dahlia, 'Park Princess'.

Echinacea – "it's all good."

Scrubbed-up spuds at the Salisbury Show.

Malus robusta 'Red Sentinel' has jellyable crab apples. Photo © Ed Sanger.

Sorbus vilmorinii – Christopher Pilking-ton's favourite rowan. Photo © Ed Sanger.

Clematis viticella 'Alba Luxurians' takes over the plum tree.

"When the autumn weather turns the leaves to flame."

Berry time in the hedgerows –
hawthorn haws.

Boston Ivy – glossy green to red.

Salisbury City Council's dazzling tulip display in Victoria Park, admired by Raffy
Moreton.

Wow, put your shades on for these colours.

Sinful.

Sinful parrot.

"What are those red things…?" *Crocosmia* 'Lucifer.'

Time to prune shrub roses like 'Bonica' – stand back and survey your victim.

My neighbour Ted's hollyhock – keep them young.

SEPTEMBER

"Mellow fruitfulness"

POOR OLD KEATS. He doesn't half get quoted and not even a fee, he's so long out of copyright.

Apples, pears, plums – September is their season. I remember the joys of scrumping. There is nothing to match the first crunchy, slightly sour, white-pipped 'Cox', or a tart 'James Grieve', furtively plucked from somebody else's tree and eaten with a chunk of mature, nay geriatric, Cheddar, or if you can find it, slightly sour, crumbly Lancashire. I can taste them now, as I write. Lay me down and let me die. **Landford Trees** list 32 different apples,

A tart 'James Grieve' with a chunk of mature cheddar. Photo © Sam Roberts.

including the above, but I doubt whether I'd recognise them if they jumped up and bit me, or the other way round.

And the **pears** … Sod's law is that the most boring – 'Conference' – is often the most prolific. I often have to support the branches with washing line props. But when I spoke the name at Braemar Lodge Residential Home, where I am a volunteer gardener, eyes lit up, and I have promised a basketful when my tree is once more weighed down, as it was last year, and the one before. Boring I may find them, but they make pretty good pear and apple chutney (see page 97). 'Conference' is happy to fertilise itself, and, if it does, comes out banana-shaped, Ed Sanger at Landford tells me, a ridiculous fact. If it has a partner it comes out, hey, pear-shaped. 'Beth', however, my other pear tree, could do with some help – she's a tiny 'William'-type pear on a tiny tree, each gone in one mouthful, or eaten by wasps, not a best buy, really. I would far rather have room for 'Williams' *Bon Chrétien*', an ugly pear with inner beauty, or *'Doyenne du Comice'*, equally run-down-your-chin juicy and a bit more handsome. Those are worth waiting for while they ripen on the kitchen windowsill. Most pear trees are grafted on a Quince A semi-vigorous root-stock, by the way, so they don't get too enormous.

Plums, now. How beautiful 'Victorias' are, egg-shaped fruit in mellow yellow with a sunset blush, though Ed warns they are "apt to crop so heavily that fruit-laden branches tear away from the trunk, leaving it open to infection." Landford Trees list this and seven more. My neighbour Beryl has an unknown pinkish plum tree, and Nicky another similar. Neither of these tastes of much, but both are delicious stewed.

What is certain is that most of these trees are easy to grow and grow quite fast. ("Except 'Cox'," said Ed, "it's a pig, with high spray requirements.") Apples are usually grafted on semi-dwarf rootstocks, named after a motorway, hang on, M26, and plums on Pixy or St Julien A, which means they are all smallish trees, about 10 to 12ft.

Fruit trees are not expensive to buy – Landford price most at £24.50 (no VAT on fruit trees) – and if you have some spare space in your garden, or even a big enough lawn, you can make an orchard. The word conjures up a vision of blossom, long grass, wild daffodils, and maybe a spotted Normandy cow. I might throw in "idyllic" if the cliché police weren't on my tail. Dare I suggest an orchard adds, ahem, flavour to a garden.

Here I have replaced a few ailing apples with new trees. But I kept three old fellows: one gnarled Rackham-style apple is now a mistletoe and *Clematis montana* tree, and every year we have to cut off a dead branch. Another, a bit younger, occasionally produces an apple, if you can reach it, has a bad case of canker, is prone to woolly aphids (dab with meths), but is host to more mistletoe, *Clematis viticella* 'Elvan' and some birdfeeders, popular with everyone including magpies. They may not function as fruit trees, but they are invaluable climbing frames and feeding stations.

The third tree is the best. Probably planted when the house was built, 75 years ago, it is my beloved plum, 'Rivers' Early Prolific.' Despite half its trunk having been blown down in some storm, it is solid as the Rock of Alcatraz, supports a 'Wedding Day' rambler and an 'Alba Luxurians' clematis, is loved by the pigeons, goldfinches, mistle thrushes and redwings, while blue tits flit through its branches and nest in its holes. And as I look up today, 8th June, it is laden with small green plums which will start to ripen in a month's time, before wasps appear, and go on falling onto the lawn in glorious purple abundance until the middle to end of August. Hold my calls. It is hard work to do something with those plums for so long. With its own white blossom in March/April, 'Wedding Day's' in June, and the clematis's in June and July, it is a tree that earns its space in spades. I recommend it, if you can find it.

Landford Trees don't do it this year, but Ashridge Trees in Castle Cary do, **support@ashridgetrees.co.uk**, and also Reads Nursery near Bungay, **plants@readsnursery.co.uk**, both are mail order only. There are a couple of other nurseries too, if you google Rivers' Early Prolific plum trees. Unlike damsons, whose fruit it somewhat resembles, you can eat the tangy plums raw, as

Loganberries – easy to grow if you have 12ft. spare on a sunnyish fence.

well as stew them, jam them and chutney them (see page 99). I am a popular neighbour, come July, when I turn up on people's doorsteps with heaped colanders.

In August I turn up on my friend Anne Johns' doorstep with colanders: her old **damson** tree just keeps on going. Last year she and her husband Bob rigged up a net to catch most of the enormous crop, which cascades into the fuchsias and all over the path. Anne makes 90 to 100 jars of jam a year for her B&B guests (see page 98), and rings people in desperation, begging them to come and take some fruit – as much as they can handle.

On from the purple passage we go to **autumn raspberries.** They need slightly less space than the summer ones, about 2 ft for each plant, and wire between posts to be tied to. Unlike July raspberries, which fruit on the previous year's canes, and you prune

Strangely attractive big yellow quinces make excellent jelly.

immediately they're over, autumn ones fruit on the current year's growth. Their yield is not as great as the summer ones, but they will go on producing raspberries from late August till the first frosts. Cut all canes to the ground in February.

Earlier in the summer I pick 'Peregrine' **peaches,** fan-trained against a west fence (August), **loganberries** 12ft wide against the same fence (June/July), dessert **gooseberries** in a west border (June/July**),** and in July too the enormous **blackcurrants,** and some **red,** at Bake Farm PYO. As for **strawberries**, the first sign of summer, I sometimes go and crawl along the rows, staining my knees, but it is hell on the arthritics, so I pick up a punnet or three from Jean at The Quick Turnover, opposite the big Tesco's in

Southampton Road, if I am going to make jam. If you grow them at home you have to contend with the unmentionables and the blackbirds, although they don't eat the wild ones, for some reason.

The more unusual fruit trees in Landford Trees' catalogue include **figs, greengages** (I await the crop of about 12 on Father Keith's young tree), **medlars, mulberries, apricots and quinces.** Last year I was able to fill a few buckets from Mrs George's quince tree, which had produced a record crop of strangely attractive big yellow fruit, and made about a dozen jars of quince jelly. It was a big tree though, and crops erratically, so I don't think I would recommend getting a young one. You can use the quinces on the Japanese quince, or chaenomeles, to make perfectly good jelly.

Let's ask the experts at Landford Trees for their choice of three fruit trees:

Ed Stanger's top three:

1. **Apple 'Red Devil':** "A crunchy self-fertile apple with a very nice flavour. Other red apples include 'Red Falstaff' and 'Red Windsor.'"

2. **Plum 'Marjorie's Seedling':** "Later picking, crops well, good flavour, can eat off the tree or cook."

3. **Pear 'Fertility':** "Russety skin, good flavour, partially self-fertile."

Christopher Pilkington's top three:

1. *Malus robusta* **'Red Sentinel':** "Pillar box red crab apples hang on right into winter, and can also be made into jelly."

2. ***Sorbus vilmorinii:*** "Rowan, or mountain ash. It starts with darkish clusters of pinky-red berries that gradually become pale pink. Lovely dark green glossy foliage."

3. ***Crataegus lavallei*** (**'Carrierei'**): "Orangey fruiting hawthorn, leaves hang on till late, berries are a wonderful colour against the dark foliage."

Thanks, again, Ed and Christopher. All these are available from

Landford Trees, Landford Lodge, Landford, Salisbury SP5 2EH. Telephone: 01794 390808
email: trees@landfordtrees.co.uk
Open: Monday to Thursday 8am to 5pm
Friday 8am to 4pm. www.landfordtrees.co.uk

——— JOBS FOR SEPTEMBER ———

- **Move or plant Oriental poppies**, to give them time to settle in before they start into growth early next year.

- **It's a prime planting month** for new things too.

- **Plant bulbs**, as many as you can of all types except tulips.

- **Start tidying up**, cutting things down and constantly deadheading.

- Make a start on **autumn lawn feeding, moss killing,** raking and tining. It probably won't make a jot of difference.

- **Prune climbing and modern rambling roses** – see Stewart's How To in November.

OCTOBER

Autumn colours

"WHEN THE AUTUMN WEATHER TURNS THE
LEAVES TO FLAME" (*September Song*), I remember
Loch Tummel in October. This is the time for that drive, through
the tunnels of beeches on the turn. The beauty of autumn leaves
seems to be a consolation for the end of summer. I did it once
with Wortle the Doberman as my passenger, stopping at view-
points to look down the loch towards the mountains, and in the
beech groves to chase sticks. The whole of Perthshire is alight in
October – it's one of the best months to visit Scotland. New

England? Phooey. What do they call it? Leaf peeping – ridiculous name. Maples, aspens, poplars and sumacs *(Rhus)* are the main stars there, but you can't beat the beech, in my opinion.

Most of us don't have the luxury of a beautiful beech, or copper beech, in our own gardens, though I'm not sure I would want such a huge tree – far better to admire those in the park, or have a hedge. We can, however, achieve a lot of colour through things like Virginia creeper and Boston ivy to climb and cling and cover, planting the tough old *Cotoneaster horizontalis,* which turns a satisfying shade of marmalade, and will grant you many arching offspring in unlikely places, including paving cracks, flame-coloured nasturtiums, and Japanese maples, *Acers,* which though slow growers, and a touch temperamental, can give you a bit of a thrill, particularly if you are young enough, have the time enough, the space enough, and acid soil enough, to grow them into proper trees.

Dear, much-missed Geoff Hamilton – no-one has taken his place on *Gardeners' World* – liked *Acer palmatum* 'Osakazuki', bright crimson, and *Acer* 'Silver Vein', warm yellow, the snakebark maple, preferably together. I think the former is the one I admired growing outside **Courtens Garden Centre** in Whiteparish, near Salisbury, so I went over there to invite the owner, **Chris Hiles,** who knows his stuff, to give me his top three favourites for autumn colour.

"Why only three?" he asked, walking me down the aisles of shrubs in his bush hat. "Look at *Hydrangea quercifolia*, the oak-leaved hydrangea, white flowers, goes purple in autumn – a big shrub, 6ft x 8ft, maybe a little tender? This *Cotinus coggygria* 'Royal Purple' is well-known, but what about 'Grace', a small tree, whose purple leaves turn brilliant red in autumn.   Or *Euonymus alatus*, the winged spindle, a small shrub, that can grow to about 6ft high over ten years, with dark green leaves going through various shades of red, to a really dark red, and it's OK on chalky soil.

"Most strong autumn colours," he went on, "are from acid-loving plants.   Some can cope with neutral soil, but they go a better colour in acid soil, with lots of light.   If you grow Japanese *Acers* in a pot, use ericaceous compost.   Try the American dogwood,

Flame-coloured nasturtiums – how can I show autumn colours in black and white?

Cornus kousa 'Celestial Shadow' – it has yellow and green variegated leaves that add red to the variegation in autumn." He showed me a photo in *Hillier Gardener's Guide to Trees and Shrubs*. "Then for climbers there's always *Vitis coignetiae*, an amazing reddish purple."

"But your top three?" I insisted. "OK," he said, grimacing.

Chris Hiles' top three trees for autumn colour:

1. *Acer palmatum* **'Osakazuki':** "For its sheer range of colour. It changes from green in the summer through purple to a fiery scarlet. A nice small tree, and you can grow it in a pot too. It is not fine-leaved, so is less susceptible to windburn from the early cold winds as the leaves unfurl, but once they have hardened off, all *Acers* can be put in full sun. Look at the one growing outside here – it has no protection, and it thrives. People are always stopping to take photographs."

(Obviously a must-have, if both Chris and Geoff recommend it.)

2. *Ginkgo biloba:* "The maidenhair tree. A big tree, can grow 100 ft high. Quite easy, very tough, and goes a buttery, clear yellow in the autumn."

3. *Rhus typhina* **'Tiger Eyes':** "Goes from limey yellow now in the summer, to a flaming red and orange. It gets to about 6ft x 6ft." "What about the suckers?" I asked, most people's objection to owning one, or having one next door. "I spray them with Roundup," Chris said, "it doesn't seem to kill the tree." (Or remove them when the tree is dormant.)

Thanks, Chris, I shall clear some space right away.

**Courtens Garden Centre, Romsey Road, Whiteparish,
Nr Salisbury, Wilts SP5 2SD. Telephone: 01794 884489
www.courtensgardencentre.co.uk
Open 7 days a week:
Summer (March to October) 9.30am to 5pm Monday to
Saturday, 10.30am to 4.30pm Sunday.
Winter (November to February) 10am to 4pm
Monday to Saturday, 10.30am to 4pm Sunday.**
They also stock loose bulbs and from January over 40 varieties of
seed potatoes. Well worth a journey if you live near Whiteparish.
Vaut le détour.

MELLOW JAM AND CHUTTINESS

Come, ye thankful people, come, raise the song of harvest-home.
All is safely gathered in. But what to do with all that fruit? As a
long-time jam maker, who revels, like one of Macbeth's witches,
in stirring a vast cauldron, eye of newt and toe of frog, wool of bat
and tongue of dog, the seductive scent of stewing plums, the
steaming up of kitchen windows, the screaming of smoke alarms,
the miracle of producing jewel-coloured jars of jam, and black-
est chutney, to stash away in the larder, I beg your indulgence if I
give you my favourite five recipes for jamming, jellying and chut-
ting. Great, cough, dare I mention it, C*******s presents?

Pear and apple chutney

About 2 kg each 'Conference' pears and apples, peeled, cored and
sliced. Put in pan with 4 cloves garlic, and a little water, cook
covered till soft. Add ½ litre malt vinegar, crystallised/stem
and/or 4 inches real shaved ginger, 1 kg brown sugar, 500g

sultanas, 1 teaspoon each mixed spice, cayenne, salt and curry paste or powder. Bring to boil, stirring until sugar is dissolved, add another ½ litre vinegar and cook till thick and rich. Pour into hot jam jars, clean around rim with Jeycloth, put on wax circles, and cellophane or foil top if using metal lid. Keep as long as you can bear, then combine with strong Cheddar on multi-seed bread for fantastic cheese and pickle doorsteps. Use bib.

Apple and mint jelly

A secret ingredient to add fruitiness to stews, this is a doddle: chuck a whole load of apples, chopped in quarters, generous bunches of mint and some water to come about half way up apples, into a pan, cover and simmer till soft. Remove mint. Mash. Drip through jelly bag overnight, and following day add just under 1 lb gran sugar to each pint of apple juice, boil to buggery till setting point is reached, let it cool for fifteen minutes, then pot in hot jars. Fantastic with cold lamb too.

Anne's damson jam

Wash fruit and weigh, then stew till soft, and mash – you don't need water. Put aside just under 1 lb gran sugar to each pound of damsons, say ¾lb. Now comes Anne's method, the clever part: squash stewed fruit, stones and all, though a colander. This avoids the endless standing over it, fishing out stones, of yesteryear, and retains most of the flesh. Jam up.

Apricot, cardamom and almond jam

Get a tray of virgin apricots, slightly unripe if poss, from the grocer. Remove stones from about half (this takes two sessions)

Rowan jelly is the best to serve with grouse and venison.
Photo © Sarah James.

and weigh apricots. Add about a pint of water, and the black seeds from 20 cardamon pods, cracked open under a tea towel with a rolling pin, and stew. When cooked, add the usual ¾lb **(jam)** sugar per lb of fruit. Stir in 2oz whole blanched almonds, and jam it up. Wonderful combination of flavours, though the almonds do look rather like fingernails, floating about. It can also be made with dried apricots – they need a bit more water.

Rivers or any plum in the oven chutney

This is easy, providing you don't mind stinking out your entire house, and possibly the whole street, with fruity curryness all night. It should take 24 hours in the lowest of ovens. At 3 in the morning once, I gave up, after nine hours, took it out, and gave it two or three hours on a low hob the next day. (It might need bringing to the boil to thicken up.)

However, if you're feeling brave, or going on holiday, preheat oven to 140C gas mark 1. Mix the following together in roasting tin: 2.3kg plums, halved and stoned, 430g raisins, 6 inches of fresh ginger, cut into matchsticks, 4 huge cloves garlic, 220g blanched split almonds, chilli powder or deseeded and chopped fresh chillies, 120g mustard seed, 1kg brown sugar, 1½ bottles white wine vinegar. Cover tightly with foil and stuff in for 24 hours, stirring occasionally. About two hours before time is up, remove foil and leave chutney to cool down slowly until most of the liquid has evaporated, to give thick, inky black, rich mixture. Irresistible. Leave to mature as long as possible.

JOBS FOR OCTOBER

- **Scarify, tine and feed lawn.** Might as well try to improve it.

- **Buy and plant new things.** The fun part.

- **Take cuttings** of anything you can find to have a go at. Buy hormone rooting gel. (See instructions in December Q & A.)

- **Start spraying apples and pears against winter moth.**

- **Start tickling up the soil** – the frost will help.

- **Order bare root roses.**

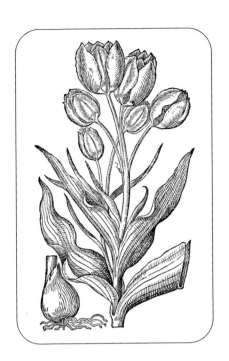

NOVEMBER

Tulips: sex on stalks

TULIPS BREAK ALL THE RULES. They can be perfectly well-behaved in colour-themed beds, pure white with green and silver ('Spring Green', 'White Triumphator'), yellow lily-flowered ('West Point') underplanted with blue forget-me-nots, purple and pink ('Burgundy', 'China Pink'), or guardsman red ('Apeldoorn', 'Red Shine'), but, unlike some other plant mixes, where more is quite often less, more tulips are definitely <u>more.</u>

I'll say. Massed in multi-coloured costumes like a chorus of can-can dancers, they flaunt it, they shout it, they lift up their frilly skirts, and tell us all about it. They show us their startling combinations, and they get abloodyway with it. This year Victoria Park had a circular bed of a dozen different kinds, the colours so bright you had to put your shades on. Good on you, Salisbury City Council – I am usually so rude about your municipal bedding.

Stripy parrots with their huge ruffled flowers, that burst upon us in May when most other tulips have faded, must be the most flamboyant of all. 'Black Parrot' now, in seductive darkest purple, with deep fringed petals, is sex on legs, or stalks. And what about 'Rococo', red and green, or the black 'Queen of the Night'? Fan me down, I am having a moment.

And when you bring them indoors, anything goes. I bought two bunches of mouth-watering orange and red parrots at Haskells in the market, and they took on another life when I got them home, brazenly arching backwards. Angela says tulips have an animal quality about them – there is more to them than just flowers. If you put them in a vase you never know what they'll do.

To dig up or not to dig? That is the question. Famous gardens (see Colin below) probably do, and replant every year. That would go in my top ten list of boring garden jobs. So in my non-famous garden I compromise: the tulips in the ground stay there, and something sinful in a pot gets thrown away after one dramatic display. These are the more exotic ones – parrots, paeony-flowered, fringed, lily-flowered, *viridiflora* – many of whose extraordinary colours are caused by a virus, which causes the majority to succumb in year two.

Have you been to Keukenhof tulip fields, easily reached from Amsterdam, to marvel at row upon row of different coloured tulips, painted by Monet? In 2013 it opens 21st March to 20th May, 8am to 7.30pm, €14,50 adults, €7 children 4 to 11. Let's all go.

Trial and error tips to plant tulips successfully:

- **Buy them loose** if you can – as big and firm as possible.

- **Keep bulbs in frost-free place** until November.

- **Dig hole twice the height of bulbs.**

- **Put a handful of bonemeal** in the bottom, and a handful of grit to help drainage.

- **Plant tulip**, pointy bit up. (Sorry.)

- **Cover and mark place** to remind you.

- If in a pot, use **John Innes No.3**, cram in as many as you can, and top with grit or broken slate.

- **Stand pot on bricks** so it can drain.

I asked Colin Hayman, Gardener in Charge of National Trust's Mompesson House, in Salisbury Cathedral Close, for his top three tulips:

"As National Trust houses open a month earlier than they used to – Mompesson on 10th March this year, closing 4th November – we have to plan tulips and other plants which start early and fill the garden with colour until it closes. Therefore I choose:

1. **'Orange Emperor':** "A *fosteriana* tulip, big terracotta orange flowers, early, late March to April."

2. **'Couleur Cardinal':** "One of the oldest commercially available that anyone can buy, deep red, flowering mid April."

3. **'Maureen':** "White, late flowering, attracts a lot of comments at Mompesson. White is a hard colour to place, but is striking *en masse,* and lasts well.

"For pots I would choose a fourth: **'Princess Irene':** dual coloured, soft orange with purple streaks, mid April. I've grown it for many years. At Mompesson we order 100 at a time, to make a big impression – around 45,000 people come through the house and garden in a year. We take them out after flowering, because we're a public garden and need to fill every inch of space, so I can't comment on whether they return year after year. I do advise ordering early, as soon as the catalogues come out, at the latest by August, in order to get the best stock and the biggest bulbs."

Thank you, Colin.

1, 2 and 4 are available in 2013 from P. De Jager & Sons Ltd, Church Farm, Ulcombe, Maidstone, Kent ME17 1DN. Telephone: 01622 840229 www.dejager.co.uk Email: flowerbulbs@dejager.co.uk 'Maureen' is not in their current catalogue, but Mr Willard at De Jager says they could get it, by special request.

Mompesson House, Choristers Green, The Close, Salisbury SP1 2EL. Telephone 01722 335659. www.nationaltrust.org/mompesson-house **Email: mompessonhouse@nationaltrust.org.uk Open: Monday, Tuesday, Wednesday, Saturday and Sunday 11am to 5pm.** It's a little gem.

Parrot tulips – if you put them in a vase you never know what they'll do.

LET'S GET PRUNING

Brace yourselves, men. We know you hate pruning, we've seen you flinch and bring your knees closer together. But we've got to do it. Why? Because if we don't, things get completely chaotically out of control. See under nature untamed in an abandoned garden, see clematises in a hopeless tangle, see *leylandii* sky high and driving the neighbours crazy, see the weak obliterated by the strong, see the diminution of flowers. See old shrubs getting older, scraggier, woodier and unhealthier. Goodness, I know the feeling. Quick, come and prune me, someone.

Let's deal with roses, as it's November, one of the two traditional rose pruning months. Why is it that pruning roses is

The old prune prunes a buddleia – hack it back ruthlessly.

something people find difficult? "I am so scared of doing the wrong thing, I daren't make a start," a friend confided, a view borne out by many of **Pococks Roses'** customers.

Let's get it straight: you can't hurt a rose. "In the wild, deer prune them", said Stewart Pocock. "Instead of nibbling it with your teeth, you are using secateurs." A rose rejoices in being pruned, it thrives on it. All you need is a pair of decent secateurs, a pair of loppers, some Flexitie cord or horrible green string, a pair of scissors to cut it with, good thick gardening gloves, and bags or a wheelbarrow for the droppings. Take these out to the roses on a warmish, sunnyish day – neither you nor they will enjoy working together in the frost.

Bush roses, shrub roses, patio and ground cover, like 'Remember Me', 'Bonica', 'Flower Power', or 'Wiltshire': the rose may be a mess of branches, some still flowering, albeit rather halfheartedly. Where to start? Stand back and survey your victim. In November all we are interested in doing is shortening it, to prevent the wind rocking the roots. You can take about a third off each branch. Go on, it won't bite. It might prick you, though, be careful, hence gloves. Take your secateurs and cut at an angle above an outward facing bud. This encourages new growth to sprout left or right, not inwards into a dark Spaghetti Junction in the middle of the bush, or a suicidal romp into the wall.

Bang, that's it. Chop up the pruned branch and bag it. Keep going. There could be quite a lot of standing back, staring, thinking, with your head on one side. Tie in any stems flapping about, and when it looks a lot tidier, congratulate yourself you have nothing more to do until mid February to mid March. In those months you will have a better skeleton to which you can bring more of a surgeon's technique, in clearing the centre of the bush, lopping off any dead wood, weedy branches, or one if two are crossing, and making the rose into an even better shape, followed by feeding, ready to rock 'n' roll to greater effect in June.

Once-flowering bush roses, like *Rosa glauca*: The God advises a slightly different approach: prune out old flowered branches, and leave the new shoots full length, i.e. thin it, not shorten.

Once-flowering ramblers, like 'Albertine': Prune after their June flowering, say in July or August. If you prune them now you'll be cutting off next year's flowers.

Climbers and modern repeat-flowering ramblers, like 'Compassion' and 'Super Fairy', are pruned in the same way, I am advised by Pococks. And in September, not November. "Fan the growth out horizontally, tying in with string. The following year you will get a lot of vertical shoots, which need cutting back to approximately ½ inch from the main horizontal stem, and any other strong growth that comes from lower down can also be trained in horizontally. We always do this when the rose has finished growing, the sap is still flowing, and the branches are still flexible. Basically you are making an espalier out of your climber. You will get many more flowers and avoid that 6ft of bare stem at the bottom. If the rose if going up a pillar, pole, obelisk or arch, spiral the strong growth around the structure." Thank you, Stewart. I have a lot of naked bottoms.

Finally, I was amused to see in the Concise Oxford Dictionary the word 'prune' (informal) can mean a disagreeable person. This old prune has doubtless killed many bushes in her time, but on balance my mantra is still: **When in doubt, chop it out.** Good luck.

JOBS FOR NOVEMBER

- **Prune roses.**

- **Order bare root roses.**

- **Plant tulips.**

- **Keep tickling up the soil,** but not if claggy and soggy.

- **Gooseberries:** cut new growth by a half, and reduce side shoots to 2 inches. Cut out dead branches, those growing into the centre, and dragging along the ground – gooseberries are lethal to try and pick there.

DECEMBER

Dig deeper - any questions?

SETTLE BACK, PUT YOUR FEET UP, and send me your gardening dilemmas. Here are some questions I've collected this year:

"When my garden looks a mess before people come to lunch, what can I do along the lines of a lick and a promise until I have time to do it later?" (Nicky)

Ha! I've heard that one before. "Time to do it later" indeed! Let me cast you one of my looks, Nicky, cruel woman that I am. Just

I scrub up to answer your questions. Bring 'em on.

get out there and tart up the bits you can see from the house. Mow the lawn, pull out the weeds, deadhead whatever needs deadheading, stick a pot of tulips or lilies or whatever's in season into a bed if you feel like it. Chances are your guests will be far too busy stuffing themselves with your famous slow roast lamb and testing bottles from Nigel's cellar to wander round the house and find the mile high 'Compassion' at the back.

"Do apples need pollinators?" (Steph)

Yes, ideally, with varieties which flower at the same time. (See Hessayon: *The Fruit Expert* for pruning groups.) But in a garden with other apple trees growing nearby you probably don't need to worry. Some, like 'James Grieve', are self-fertile. Pears, yes. Best to buy a pollination partner, as it's rather attractively called, since fewer people grow pears. See Hessayon again.

"When daffodils come up blind, will they always be blind?" (George)

Yes. Unless you dig them up, separate the small bulbs attached to the parent, replant and wait patiently for them to get big enough to flower. Overcrowding is why good daffodils turn bad, and unless you have spare space and a lot of patience, it's probably best to give them the old heave-ho after any in the group have flowered (keep that one), and start again. Daffodils are not expensive and drooping leaves are a depressing sight. Fling 'em out.

"How do you incorporate the practical workings of a garden, ie the shed, greenhouse, compost bins?" (Joel)

Steph answered this one: "In grand gardens they have plenty of space to hide them. In more normal ones, expose them with pride. Paint the shed a jolly colour, put bins in a trellis enclosure and grow clems up it. Personally I rather like a greenhouse."

"How do I get my bank looking like that?" (Steph, looking at the M8 verges covered in oxeye daisies.)

Read Christopher Lloyd's *Meadows*, he's the expert. But as for oxeye daisies, clear some space in the grass and chuck a packet of seeds down. They're such survivors they might struggle through, and once you've got them, you've got them forever. As for these "Meadow Mixes", I am unconvinced. Four people I know have tried, and four have failed.

"How do you stop lavender going woody?" (Julie)

Chop it back twice a year: after flowers have faded, cut stems back to base, and in March go over the bush with secateurs or a hedge trimmer, cutting off about an inch to two inches more. You can't prevent it going woody, but this will slow woodiness down and keep it in a better shape. Be careful not to cut into the old wood – you might kill it. Lavenders have a limited lifespan, though (see Alan's advice in July), so you might need to grit your teeth, dig them up and start again if they get too geriatric.

"Do gooseberries need mates?" (Sue)

What is this obsession you all have with sex and fruit trees? I looked it up, but neither Hessayon nor my ancient vegetable book says anything about pollination. So I rang Courtens Garden Centre. "No", answered Heather. "You can have just one gooseberry bush, and it'll fruit fine."

"What are those red things and how do I grow them?" (Andrea)

Crocosmia 'Lucifer', and you just shove 'em in somewhere sunny. Be brave with numbers, if you've got room – five, seven or nine make a really good flamboyant display. They come out in July and morph into interesting seed heads in August. Nice sword-like leaves. They used to be called montbretia and they used to be orange and I used to hate them. But in red it's a totally different animal. Go for it.

"Can I take a cutting off a bay tree?" (John)

Yes, a semi-ripe cutting in the summer. Pull off a young stem with a 'heel' or cut off with secateurs, put immediately into a plastic bag to prevent transpiration, strip off lower leaves, cut below a leaf node, dip bottom in hormone rooting gel and plant in a gritty compost, or one mixed with Perlite. Water and leave in not too sunny a place outdoors. Same principle applies to lavender, sage and rosemary. I usually trim the top off these as well, so the cutting can concentrate its energies on rooting.

"How can I stop the buggers eating my hostas?" (Gus)

Grit, copper tape, eggshells, coffee grounds, bran, beer … we've all been there, and it seems to boil down to the dreaded blue pellets and clearing up the corpses. But the other day Jonathan Leiserach rang me, and said had I heard about Blu-Tack? Apparently they don't like crossing it. Try anything once – I shall experiment by scrunching it round the rim of one of mine in a pot. Let me know if you do and how it goes.

"How can I create colour with self-supporting tall plants?" (Vanessa)

A few, like *Verbena bonariensis*, or the oaty *Stipa gigantea,* and other grasses, stand up on their own, but others need tactful support, at an early stage of growth. We were looking at your pink Japanese anemones at the time, at least as high as we were. You can buy the rusty iron interlocking supports mentioned in the July chapter on the herbaceous border at Longstock Park Nursery over there, or similar elsewhere. Semi-circular ones are good too, to hold in things like *Cephalaria gigantea*. A visit to the nursery will give you some good ideas.

"What can I plant in the shade by my hedge, preferably a colourful hardy perennial?" (Anne)

Try Japanese anemones, or 'Canary Bird' yellow rose or lavender clematis, 'Perle D'Azur', periwinkles. All these grow well in the shade, though it would be useful if the rose got a bit of sun. The Japanese anemones will grow taller if in the sun, but they're still OK in shade. Not that colourful, but utterly reliable, is the faithful *Euonymus* 'Green and Gold', a variegated shrub which brightens up the darkest corner, and I grow *Mahonia japonica* perfectly happily. In spring, go for hellebores and bulbs, of course, of all sorts – snowdrops, bluebells, *Scillas*.

"What is the best height arrangement in a border? Should one go for a gradual rise in height to the wall or is it better to mix short and tall? I'm sure the meanest gardener knows these things, but I ask as a complete novice." (Anne)

It used to be conventional to put low things at the front and gradually rise up – and that still works well. But there are also a number of tall but transparent flowers, like fennel and *Verbena bonariensis*, which can go anywhere, particularly growing through grasses like *Stipa arundinacea*. The Longstock Park herbaceous border (see July) is a great example of mix it all up a bit – it has a huge clump of waist-high blue agapanthus at the front of one bed, and waving about thigh-high white *Gaura* 'Whirling Butter-flies', at the front of another. Big things are generally at the back, but the Giant's Causeway mixture adds a bit more excitement. Basically, Anne, anything goes. Try everything.

"What is the best time to move a young hydrangea that's in the wrong place?" (Caroline)

I was about to say in the autumn, but as the hydrangea might still be in flower then, I'd wait till the spring. When the ground is not frozen, from March onwards, give the hydrangea a good drink, dig a hole in not too sunny a spot, sprinkle bonemeal, fill up with water and let drain, dig up the plant with a generous amount of earth around it, shove in, lightly stamp down, water again, and pray. You could prune it at the same time, if it needs it.

"Pruning seems to be a minefield, especially when it comes to shrubs. Is there a general rule that one can follow, or must I continue to look up each one individually (difficult when the name escapes me)?" (Daphne)

In general terms we prune early summer shrubs (up to end of June) immediately they've stopped flowering – ceanothus, forsythia, kerria, philadelphus. That allows them to get on with making new growth, and hardening it off, before the first frosts.